Diving
in Darkness

Beneath rock, under ice,
into wrecks

Martyn Farr

Assisted by Pat Cronin
Foreword by Jill Heinerth

WILD PLACES
CARDIFF

WILD PLACES PUBLISHING
51 TIMBERS SQUARE
CARDIFF CF24 3SH, UK

First published 2003

Overhead environment diving is a potentially hazardous undertaking
that exposes a diver to considerable risk if practised incorrectly or with
incomplete planning or procedures; it requires training, adequate
equipment and experience. This book is not intended as a substitute for
any of these factors, but is a source of information on diving beneath
ice, within wrecks and in flooded caves and mines, or similar underwater situations where there is no direct access to an air surface.
Anyone intending to enter these environments should first become a
fully proficient open water diver. This book assumes a basic knowledge
of diving technique and knowledge and should be used to complement a
training course specialising in the overhead environment.

It is not possible to explain or demonstrate every element of potential
hazard or risk within the scope of this text and neither the author nor
publisher accepts any responsibility or liability for any loss, damage or
injury, including death, howsoever caused, which may result from
actions undertaken after reading this book. The inclusion of any named
dive site should not be taken to mean that access is freely available and
in all cases appropriate permission must be sought.

British Library Cataloguing in Publication Data
A catalogue record for this book is available from the British Library

ISBN 0-9526701-5-1

Design and origination by Wild Places Publishing, Cardiff
Printed on Black Label Satin, a paper manufactured from sustainable
  sources
Printed in the United Kingdom by Haven Colourprint, Pembroke Dock

CONTENTS

Acknowledgements

IT has taken over three years to compile this basic guide to overhead environment diving. Throughout every stage my good friend Patrick 'Pat' Cronin has been of great assistance, quietly suggesting, supporting and critically evaluating the book's direction and content.

For diagrams and computer imaging I am indebted to Chris Howes, John Parker and Jenny Pinder, and for many valuable suggestions on all aspects of the final production I must thank Judith Calford.

Perry Suojoki offered first-hand information and constructive criticism on ice diving, as did Canadian Jill Heinerth. Her exploration of caves is extensive, including Wakulla Springs as part of the US Deep Caving Team where her cave dives took her deeper than any woman in history. She was inducted into the Women Divers Hall of Fame, named Canadian Technical Diver of the Year and in 2001 Jill and her husband Paul were the first people to cave dive inside an iceberg. I am particularly indebted to Jill for commenting on the draft text and writing the foreword for *Diving in Darkness*.

The table of dive times related to oxygen partial pressures on p61 is based on data published by the National Oceanic and Atmospheric Administration (NOAA). José de Veer supplied the dive profile on p64.

Finally, for long, gruelling hours, often beyond the bounds of patience and in cold, inhospitable environments, I must credit my primary photographic assistants: Pat Cronin and Phil Dotchon. Without Phil's practical expertise many trips would have foundered at a very early stage. Phil: you are the Mr Fix-it wizard.

Photography

Unless otherwise stated all photographs are by the author, who is grateful to the following divers for generously supplying additional images:

Leigh Bishop: pp115, 116, 117, 118, 121, 127
Pat Cronin: back cover
Jill Heinerth: pp7, 109, 110, 112b
Chris Howes: pp26t, 29t, 32, 34b, 36, 37t, 38, 41, 47 (top row), 49, 50b, 51b, 52r, 53r, 63r, 71, 78, 85, 122, 123, 124, 125, 126
Peik Joutsen: p114m
Jaakko Junno & Jaakko Nurmela: p104
Jouni Polkko: pp43, 108, 111, 112t, 113, 114t&b
Ken Sullivan: p119

Entering Nascente do Rio Formoso (Formoso Springs), Bonito, Brazil

Foreword

by Jill Heinerth

WE had been submerged for over two hours in water at −1.6°C. The depth was just shy of 40m and our waiting vessel was 300m back through the ice cave in a rapidly accelerating current. My husband and I saw the blue glow of an alternative exit and decided to hedge our bets and make an easy swim out. We surfaced in glaring Antarctic sunshine over a kilometre from our ship, on the blind side of a massive iceberg we called Ice Island Cave #4. I grumbled and pulled out an orange surface marker buoy and thought about the unpleasant pros-

Jill Heinerth on a Cis-Lunar rebreather at −45m, heading into Wakulla Springs, Florida, and (below) preparing the rebreather for use

pects of drifting in pack ice towards New Zealand. In the summer eternal daylight, at least we stood a good chance of being spotted by our vessel even at the late hour. We had been the first people to cave dive the interior lattice of an iceberg and now all I could hope for was a chance to tell the story.

On the way home from Antarctica the expedition crew sat down for a celebratory meal and shared our 'most frightening' experiences from the trip, each person telling his or her personal story. For the captain it was the night we 'almost sank'. For the helicopter pilot it was the discovery that we would have to rebuild the chopper's corroded electronics after crossing the Southern Ocean. For my husband, it was the moment he was almost crushed between pack ice and the stern of our vessel. For other divers, it was the daunting vertical currents that tried to suck them into the depths; for scientists, it was the long periods when we were frozen in place and unable to move the ship. Still others recalled rogue waves over 20m high and the roll of the vessel over fifty degrees to starboard. It was a dangerous mission and we had faced many difficulties along the way.

To most, our stories would appear unbelievable; our goals and decisions complete lunacy. But, as we shared our tales, a unique trend evolved. Most stories involved a completely private experience of the dangers that we had faced. In many cases the events were a revelation to those not involved. I was never aware that we almost sank during the night, or that my husband was fending off house-sized chunks of pack ice as he awaited his lift back onto our vessel. The greatest risks were almost always faced and solved alone, and the stories were far less frightening to the individual involved – who had the experience and the proper tools to deal with the issues he or she faced.

PEOPLE have asked me how I became involved in such apparently dangerous pursuits – just as every mother will ask each reader of this book about their motivations when diving beneath an overhead environment.

When I teach a cave or wreck diving class, I always ask my students about their motivation for signing up. Some answers are well defined, while other divers discover that their motive is not worth the risk involved. Risk assessment and assumption is the most critical skill needed for survival, but that has to be tempered with patience. Experienced cave diver Dr Bill Stone once told me that to be a good explorer, when things don't go according to plan within a hair's width of your goal, you need to be able to step back, abort the mission and say to yourself, 'No, not today – not yet.'

The second pair of crucial survival skills are problem-solving and critical thinking. Although some may think that over-learned motor skills are the secret to dealing with challenges underwater, I would argue that emergencies are rarely black and white. When faced with an air emergency, calm, critical thinking may reveal that a slow and deliberate exit from the cave is the best option, instead of a fast sprint that might deplete the team's gas reserves. In the event of a lost teammate, exiting to arrange back-up support may be more prudent than searching beyond safe reserves. Each emergency is individual and learned responses have to be supplemented with calm, critical thinking.

Closely allied with critical thinking is the skill of restraint. It is easy for a new diver to be consumed by enthusiasm. In modern times we expect instant gratification for our efforts, but good technical divers understand that there is no substitute for time in the water. With time comes experience, and with experience come character building situations and better critical thinking.

As I built my personal foundation in technical diving I became ravenous for information. In the late 1980s very few Canadians were involved in technical diving and information and instructors were scarce. The word 'nitrox' was mumbled in hushed tones in the back of dive shops and twinsets were viewed as sacrilege. Luckily, that forced my research into a truly international quest. I was deeply influenced by Martyn's *The Darkness Beckons*, published in 1980, which revealed a marvellous legacy of people from all over the world who had and were independently solving the issues they faced in exploration. Through his book I saw that curious people pursued a variety of techniques and tools to achieve their goals. I learned that an open mind and critical thinking would allow me to do the same.

Martyn's newest text carries on that tradition. He has spent time to carefully research and present a banquet of tools and approaches without casting judgement on which is correct or which is careless. Instead, he hopes that you will feast from the materials and forge your own direction as explorers beneath an overhead environment – if there was a

Paul Heinerth diving
below Antarctic pack ice

The superbly atmospheric entrance to Cenote Naharon, Riviera Maya, Mexico

perfect answer and an ideal technique, then we could not truly be called explorers.

We do not engage in exploration to merely seek thrills and gain control over mother nature. Rather, we embark on a pursuit to increase our understanding of her wonders in the last finite frontiers of this earth. Cave exploration is a puzzle. Discoveries have nothing to do with competition or ego gratification. Those who engage in exploration understand that it is a personal journey fuelled by a thirst for knowledge and adventure. It is a privilege to share the excitement of discovery with others and to be elated by the accomplishments of colleagues.

Martyn has created a resource where one can explore options and begin a personal quest of discovery and learning. In a world where many demand stock answers and militaristic conformity, that is a daunting challenge. He invites thoughtful discussion, creativity and versatility. He lays out the background and then suggests study, experience and critical thinking. His legacy of writing and photography has created a vital archive for those who seek information and his body of work demonstrates his creed: that in life's journey, it is far more satisfying to search and strive than to wither in unfulfilled dreams.

The overhead environment is not for everyone but, for those of us that built clubhouses in closets and dug tunnels in the snow, it is a magical world. Wrecks are full of rich history and caves represent one of the last frontiers of science. It is a rare privilege to dive in those environments and, whether you choose to simply peer in the threshold or use high technology to penetrate the unknown, do so with an open mind and a careful step, so that others may follow, learn and share in your wonderment.

Jill Heinerth, April 2003
Cave Diving Instructor, NSS-CDS
Technical Cave Diver Instructor and Rebreather Instructor, IANTD

Introduction

IN recent years great advances have been made in all aspects of underwater activity. There can be no doubt that in terms of equipment, techniques and training, diving is infinitely safer today than it was a generation ago. It is natural, therefore, that increasing numbers of people are extending their personal horizons. Cavern and cave diving, wreck, mine and ice penetration; these are the new frontiers and are together termed the overhead environment.

For many divers this esoteric world offers a wondrous, deep and fulfilling experience and *Diving in Darkness* will make your entry into this environment safer and more accessible, dispelling the myths that surround the subject. Particular attention is given to the essentials of the activity: there are real lessons to learn and new techniques to follow.

It is a basic requirement that divers will have achieved at least the equivalent of PADI Advanced Open Water Diver, BSAC Sports Diver or CMAS Two Star before embarking upon overhead environment training. It is stressed that thorough training by qualified instructors is essential; no book or training manual alone will ever serve this purpose. *Diving in Darkness* assumes that the reader is familiar with basic diving equipment and is competent to dive in open water. In addition, diving is a dynamic activity; there is continuous evolution in all respects of equipment and technique. As such, this book cannot claim to be a definitive study of overhead environment diving, nor is it a training manual. It aims to provide an overall awareness of the activity and to guide the reader in safe principles and approaches. You do not have to be trimix certified or a 'technical' diver to gain an insight to this new world; you must, however, be competent in basic techniques. This book does not say: 'You must do . . . this or that.' It does say, 'Keep an open mind.' Be prepared to consider new ideas and incorporate these into your diving practice, as and when required.

Overhead environment diving is becoming more popular, especially in areas such as the Yucatán peninsula of Mexico, and increasing numbers of people are enrolling on specialist courses or participating in leisure tours

Just as you trained to dive in the first place, so too must you undertake specialised training for this new realm. It is not difficult, just different. This training is more about environmental awareness and attitude than physiology, laws of physics or mathematics. Yes, there are new techniques that must be adopted but, compared with those early experiences that we all found uncomfortable, such as mask clearing, these new approaches are easily accommodated. In the same way as most divers begin their training in the relative safety of a warm swimming pool, you should be introduced to this new realm gradually, progressively and cautiously. There are no excuses for undertaking sporting activities in a reckless, irresponsible manner – the equipment, proven techniques, information and training are all readily available.

The nature of the overhead environment requires that appropriate diving techniques are used. Programmes relating to cavern and cave diving

This spectacular view of the entrance to Cenote Carwash, near Tulum in Quintana Roo, Mexico, conveys the magic of cave diving in the Yucatán peninsula

are now undertaken worldwide, though the course content varies depending upon the region and training organisation. With due respect to the smaller organisations that exist in many countries, it is true to say that the majority of these courses have been substantially influenced by the two organisations which have grown to prominence in Florida: the Cave Diving Section of the National Speleological Society and the National Association for Cave Diving. This has been due, in large measure, to the attractive nature of Florida's freshwater springs, which are diveable year round. These organisations, and those such as the Cave Diving Group of Great Britain and the Cave Divers Association of Australia, have for many years been proactive in their struggle to ensure continued access to sites and to promote a responsible attitude towards training. With the growth in popularity of diving generally, other organisations such as NAUI and PADI, and more recently TDI, IANTD and GUE, have also entered this field of training (contact information and full names for these associations appear in Appendix B).

So what is cavern diving? The term was coined in the USA for exploration in the threshold, entrance area of a flooded cave. It has today acquired a completely different meaning from that found in a dictionary or glossary of 'dry' caving – cavern diving is considered to be elementary, introductory diving in an underground tunnel, a definition which has gained international acceptance in the wider diving world. Courses are formulated to permit open water divers to experience a brief, safe exposure to the mysterious world of the flooded cave, with a minimum investment in either training or equipment. However, it is stressed that a cavern course, and the accompanying certification, does *not* constitute training for cave diving.

The limits of cavern diving are conceptually clear. They are determined by the availability of direct daylight within the cavern or by the diver's ability to make a direct ascent to the surface. As originally conceived for the clear, freshwater springs of Florida there were also minimum levels of visibility at the start of the dive and restrictions to a maximum penetration of 60m from the surface and a recommended maximum depth of 22m. The dive was not to go beyond any restriction in the passage where two divers could not pass side by side, or involve obligatory decompression.

Cavern courses are conducted in many countries, with local environmental conditions requiring minor differences in their structure. Cave diving courses, however, vary considerably. You should therefore maintain an open mind as you read the advice contained in *Diving in Darkness* and select your equipment, techniques and training as appropriate

to the type of diving or project that you have in mind; you may have knowledge of cave diving gained in one region of the world, but elsewhere different techniques may apply.

When you train in this new medium your specialist instructor will cover the techniques you must master. These will be specific to the environment you are diving in, such as beneath ice or in caves; if you subsequently transfer to a different environment you should modify your approach accordingly. Even with considerable experience in one area or environment, divers may not be competent in another or able to easily transfer their expertise to a different sphere without further training. Divers must reflect very carefully upon their experience and the training they have undertaken: address any deficiencies before embarking upon a project in a new situation. Closely study the relevant manuals in Appendix A to ensure that you are thoroughly conversant with the inherent differences in the many forms of overhead environment before you undertake the activity.

Whether taking a cavern course or advanced instruction for diving in the overhead environment, there's a great deal of fun to be had while training

Warnings such as this 'STOP' sign, placed by the NSS-CDS inside Devil's Eye Spring, north Florida, advise inexperienced divers to go no further; they are being installed in a number of popular sites

Regardless of your sporting background, the recommended training path is to progress from Cavern Diver, through Introductory Cave Diver (and perhaps Apprentice Diver in the USA), before becoming a Full Cave Diver. Divers with a good 'technical' background, for example individuals competent and experienced in using mixed gas, may access a slightly shorter, more intensive route. However, events have shown that until divers have progressed through the full training programme they should be extremely wary of conducting anything other than the most limited of dives, preferably under supervision. It is for this reason that divers at the introductory level are frequently restricted to using a single cylinder; if they dive with a twinset they are limited to a penetration during which they consume one-sixth of their air, not the one-third that is regarded as the norm at Full Cave Diver.

Prudent individuals will reflect carefully that training and qualifications will only take the diver so far. Indeed, gaining certification such as Full Cave Diver is not to be regarded as a green light allowing you to embark upon some major exploration. Conversely, it is the point where the student must take stock and consider very carefully all future dives. It is the stage where a dependence upon others should end, where the diver must assume complete responsibility for all his or her actions. Certification at this level is perhaps better considered as a licence to begin gathering experience, rather than an invitation to dive anywhere you choose in the overhead environment.

Whatever your reasons for taking up diving in an overhead environment, perhaps an attraction to explore wrecks or the enticement of unknown cave passages, your experience will be both fascinating and thrilling. Above all, however much enjoyment you derive, think clearly and dive safely.

Chapter one
The Overhead Environment

THE overhead environment – where there is a 'ceiling' or solid roof above the diver's head – encompasses several different activities. Not forgetting that deep diving presents its own 'virtual' ceiling and might be considered part of the overhead environment, in this book we are looking specifically at places where direct ascent to the surface is impossible – that is, in caves, mines, tunnels, wrecks and beneath ice.

Divers have long been attracted by the wealth of sunken wrecks to be explored and there are innumerable publications describing wreck diving. Entry to a wreck, at any depth, must be undertaken with utmost caution; apart from the threat of silt obscuring visibility, the structure will be deteriorating and quietly settling, making it an extremely hazardous place for the inexperienced. Ice diving holds its own dangers, where the temperature of the water not only poses a severe constraint upon body functions but also upon equipment. This specialist area of diving activity again requires considerable forethought and research. Like wreck penetration, the most common cause of fatality beneath the ice lies with the diver becoming lost.

Caverns, caves, mines and tunnels form the major part of the overhead environment. Activities under these conditions are significantly different from anything experienced during initial dive training where the idea is established that ultimately, in the event of trouble, an open water diver can ascend quickly to reach the surface and safety.

Clearly, if there is a solid roof above the diver's head an emergency ascent is not an option. Indeed, before a final ascent is possible it might be

A very quiet day at the easily accessible Devil's Eye Spring, part of the Ginnie Springs Dive Center near High Springs, Florida

necessary to travel horizontally for quite some distance, or even descend to a greater depth. These facts present a number of implications.

With no air surface immediately available in the event of crisis, inflating a buoyancy compensator or dropping a weight belt is not a viable proposition. To be held firmly against the ceiling of a structure by positive buoyancy, be it the roof of a cave, mine, wreck or the underside of a sheet of ice, is extremely disturbing. Whatever the original problem was that caused the emergency is now almost certainly compounded; it is highly probable that the outcome will be catastrophic. We shall look at this topic later, when we consider appropriate equipment, techniques and the effects of stress.

On entering an overhead environment the intensity of natural light rapidly drops; within a short distance there is normally no available

Piccaninnie Ponds, in the Mount Gambier region of South Australia, issues some of the clearest water on earth. Permission from the state authorities is required to dive here and there is a depth restriction of 36m

Exploration in the cenotes of Quintana Roo, Mexico, emphasises the need for archaeological conservation. Here, an ancient Mayan pot is being recorded in Cenote Dos Pisos

light at all. The difficulties of diving in darkness may be further hindered by poor visibility and, commonly, disturbed sediment. Divers often fail to appreciate that the sediment which is clearly visible on the floor of a dive site is also found on the ceiling and walls. Exhaled breath will frequently bring down a fine mud cloud, or percolation as it is known in the USA, which normally occludes the water behind the swimming diver. Crystal clear conditions on the way into a tunnel can reduce to blackout, or 'silt-out', within a very short time. It is difficult enough contending with a reduction in visibility, without exacerbating the problem! At such times orientation becomes a prime concern and thought processes are dominated by the question: 'Which way is out?'

Early in open water dive training the concept of buddy diving is instilled – of a partner being on hand to assist if anything untoward occurs. When two divers are in complete intuitive harmony (which is rare) there is no doubt that physically and psychologically they are immensely beneficial to each other. There is no question that a difficulty shared may be a problem prevented, but this buddy system can and does break down. This risk cannot be afforded in an overhead environment.

As we shall see, there are different approaches to dealing with these problems around the world. If you are in a dense silt cloud when a crisis develops your buddy may be of no help at all; indeed, your fellow diver may be totally unaware that you are in trouble. Because it is clear that there is no 'aim-for-the surface' bail-out facility, it follows that a diver in an overhead environment must be capable of solving problems as soon as they arise: divers must be self-contained and self-reliant. This can only be ensured by receiving appropriate training and carrying redundant equipment.

These principles are crucial to survival in a life-threatening scenario: you must always have the necessary equipment to deal with a problem, know exactly what to do with it and how to react to the emergency. Problems must be tackled quickly and effectively; in the overhead environment, time is not on your side.

Accident analysis

An analysis of past cave, mine and wreck-diving fatalities indicates that a number of common factors are involved:

1. Lack of training and awareness of the environment
2. Lack of, or problems with, a guideline
3. Mismanagement of air reserves
4. Depth
5. Lighting or other equipment problems

In the 1960s and '70s it was realised that a significant number of fatalities were occurring in the overhead environment, worldwide, and that many of the deceased had received no specialised training. An extreme example comes from England where, in 1970, a young 'would-be' cave diver bought his equipment one day, dived the next and disappeared. The body of Alan Erith was not found and recovered until almost five years later.

In the USA many divers have perished in the enticing waters of the Florida springs, where it was not only untrained divers but experienced and even certified instructors who came to grief. Easily accessible sites, such as Little River Springs, seemed to create an overwhelming desire to see what was 'just a little further' down the passage. The individuals concerned may have anticipated obvious hazards such as the presence of a ceiling and total darkness, but they clearly failed to appreciate the special requirements that the overhead environment brings. If their training had been appropriate and effective, and the individuals had demonstrated a mature, responsible attitude, by far the majority of incidents would never have occurred.

In comparison, there are few fatalities today. By and large the lessons have been learned. However, a disturbing trend continues with experienced divers who, for whatever reason, swim beyond the limits of their training and simply bite off more than they can chew.

The cave environment

A cave is, by definition, a naturally occurring opening or passage into the earth's crust. Caves are found in various rock strata and originate by different natural processes. The following section offers a brief overview of the subject and it is strongly recommended that anyone intent upon progressing from the limited exposure to caves gained from an introductory cavern and overhead environment course should study the relevant manuals, which are published for both cavers and divers. Understanding the specific environment is your key to safety; only when this has been achieved can you adopt appropriate equipment and dive plans.

The basic types of caves can be categorised as:

- Coral caves
- Sea caves
- Lava tubes
- Solution caves

In areas of extreme low temperature (at high latitude and/or altitude) caves also develop beneath glaciers.

Coral caves are found in tropical marine environments, are mostly short and often confined. Owing to the profusion of marine life and their small size they deserve and demand respect, in particular from accidental damage: without care, divers can unwittingly destroy much of value.

Preparing for a cave dive

Sea caves are common in many rocky cliffs, but relatively few attain any significant length or merit recreational diving (though exceptions are caves which formed millennia ago when the sea lay at lower levels, such as at St Kilda in Scotland and possibly some sites in the Bahamas). Sea caves are normally formed by the hydraulic action of waves battering upon cracks or other geological weaknesses. Owing to the severe surge or scouring effect of currents, diving into flooded sea caves may be impractical or prohibitively dangerous at some tide levels. Local advice is invaluable.

Lava tubes are much less common than either coral or sea caves, but they are often of significant length and provide fascinating opportunities. Lava tubes form in areas of volcanic activity where lava flows down a slope, the surface forms a crust and the molten rock subsequently drains to leave an open passage. The tube therefore forms above water, but when ocean levels rose following the last glacial period some were flooded. Most lava tubes are formed in basalt rock, which varies in colour between dark grey and black, and this absorbs more light than most other caves. Apart from the general gloom, these sites are frequently characterised by sharp rocks and many contain quantities of fine silt. The best known lava tubes explored by divers lie in the Canary Islands and Hawaii.

Solution caves are by far the most common caves in the world and are also the most extensive. They are formed by the action of water which has, over many thousands of years, dissolved passages in soluble carbonate rocks, generally referred to as limestone.

The precise manner of cave formation is complex, but it is important to

Cave divers may be privileged to find beautifully decorated caverns. Cova des Pas de Vallgornera, Mallorca

understand those factors which have a direct bearing upon diving. To form a cave the flow of water must be sufficiently aggressive to both erode the rock (rainwater is, effectively, a mild carbonic acid) and carry away the resulting solute and debris.

Water cannot flow directly through limestone, as it might through porous chalk or soil; instead, it trickles through an intricate, naturally occurring network of cracks and fissures. A vertical crack is known as a joint while a horizontal division between rock layers is called a bedding plane. Water will eventually enlarge a joint to produce a tall, narrow passage, while a bedding plane forms a low, wide passage; due to their restricted nature, either may require the use of side-mounted diving apparatus.

Another form of passage is oval-shaped and often referred to as a

This committing squeeze, aptly named The Birth Canal, is part of the normal entry route to a well-decorated underwater passage in McCavity Cave, near Wellington in New South Wales, Australia

phreatic tube; it is by far the most pleasant to dive through and is the preferred option (if there is one). Phreatic tubes are often found where joints and bedding planes intersect, while caverns and chambers (or rooms, as they are sometimes known) are generally found where two major fissures intersect. Their floors are frequently littered with boulders which have collapsed from the roof.

Other important terminology relates to cave entrances. Water emerges from the subterranean world at a resurgence. Wookey Hole in Somerset and Keld Head in North Yorkshire are classic examples in the UK, as is Piccaninnie Ponds in South Australia. Sites in Florida such as Wakulla Springs and Ginnie Springs are substantial freshwater resurgences (in Florida resurgences are known as springs) and form some of the largest outflows on earth. The water surface at such a spring may be characterised by a 'boil', or mushroom effect, showing clear evidence of the strong upwelling current. Diving here means swimming upstream against the flow. Generally, visibility is clearer than at sites where water flows into the ground, certainly for the inward journey before silt may have been disturbed. There is one direct environmental safety advantage – the outward dive is assisted by the current.

Water flows into the earth, or a cave, at a sink. Where a sink is flooded, as in Florida, it is often referred to as a siphon (in France this term is synonymous with sump – a flooded passage within a cave).

The identifying characteristics of a sink are very different from those of springs. The surface of the pool may exhibit a whirlpool effect where small scuds of foam, leaves or twigs rotate slowly in a circular pattern. There may be significant accumulations of other debris, such as tree trunks or domestic refuse, attesting to much higher water levels in times of flood. Sinks are referred to as downstream sites and must be approached with infinitely greater caution. There are major implications for air management and general safety, where current, visibility and possibly debris swept into the cave during floods may all serve to complicate and severely compromise a normal approach to the dive.

Some caves may have both a spring and a sink at opposite sides of the same pool; others may reverse their flow in certain seasons; in these instances it is extremely important to plan accordingly. Other caves may not demonstrate any flow whatsoever on the surface of the water and may have different terms applied to them – in Florida they are commonly known as karst window systems. These are perhaps better thought of as 'connections' to an underlying water conduit; they are frequently deep, often have a distinct cone of debris directly beneath the entrance and may exhibit an 'hourglass' profile. Not all shafts lead to a flowing network; some sinkholes are merely deep, terminal holes.

Flooded cave systems may be referred to by different names. In Mexico the spectacular caves of the Yucatán are called cenotes; in the Bahamas the openings that intermittently ebb and flow with tidal changes are called blue holes.

Completely flooded sections of passage also exist in predominantly 'dry' cave systems. Water was originally responsible for their formation and many, if not most, caves possess sections which are permanently water filled, regardless of the season; these are known as sumps. Because exploring these sites involves a host of caving skills, quite apart from dive skills, activity here is less common than on the surface. Not only are there obvious difficulties in transporting fragile diving equipment to the dive site, but the environmental conditions are frequently muddy, confined and cold. Merely to reach the dive base a series of obstacles may need to be overcome: deep shafts, raging waterfalls or dangerously unstable terrain.

Likewise, visibility within caves can be very poor. Much of the published literature, and certainly that from the USA, draws a clear distinction between such diving and that undertaken directly from the surface. Diving in 'dry' caves in the Americas is referred to as 'sump diving' where, quite often – as elsewhere in the world – the aim is to discover and explore further dry cave that may lie beyond the watery barrier. However, this subtle distinction is but a matter of words. There is little doubt that all diving in caves involves the same objective dangers, to a greater or lesser degree.

Water properties and quality

The environment determines the nature of the water at the dive site and the sediments which may be present; both must be considered by the diver.

Following the line, attached to a projecting rock using a snoopy loop (see p50), in Fontaine de Truffe, Dordogne, France

Water is not always clear; it may, for example, be characterised by light brown tannic acid, derived naturally from roots, wood and other organic debris. Some sites contain water laced with hydrogen sulphide, a product of bacterial action – the water typically exhibits a rotten egg smell and a layered zone of bad visibility. Differences in salinity in parts of a dive cause few problems, but a halocline may occur at the interface between fresh water above and salt water below. While the halocline may be limited in vertical extent, it is difficult to see clearly within it due to refraction. Lastly, varying levels of flow and perhaps pollution require consideration; these may affect visibility and both can generate stress.

Cave-bearing rocks differ greatly – Little River Springs in Florida have formed in creamy coloured strata, while dark limestones are typical of the UK. More important to the diver are the passage size and nature and quantity of silt that may be present. Silt comprises anything from sand, which settles quickly when disturbed, through mud to fine clays, the last of which can take many hours to subside. A very fine sediment consisting of decomposed organic matter, common in caves close to the sea, is known as 'mung'. Sediments often coat the walls and ceiling and the greatest care must be taken to minimise disturbance to reduce the risk of a total loss of visibility on the return dive. Flood debris, such as leaves and grass, can also be particularly troublesome.

The mine environment

Caves and mines are often synonymous terms to the open water diver. However, they are quite different: caves occur naturally while mines are man-made and contain different hazards.

Flooded mines must be considered potentially unstable. The diver in Holme Bank Chert Mine, near Bakewell in Derbyshire (above), has stayed well away from the suspect stone pillar that supports the roof, but exhausted air bubbles can nevertheless form pockets that can disturb the rock (opposite, bottom), and the problem of rotting timbers is clearly seen in the picture of Wigpool Iron Mine in the Forest of Dean (opposite, top).

The photograph on this page was taken in 1976. The diver is carrying a knife on his leg, a fundamental error as in this position it can easily snare the line and lead to entanglement

Throughout the world a tremendous variety of minerals have been extracted by man during the course of history and, owing to changing fortunes in the associated industries, many complex and extensive mines are today abandoned and flooded. As with caves, divers must develop a healthy understanding of the environment.

Mines were excavated for economic motives and as the primary concern was extracting some valuable commodity, the cheapest means possible were used. The techniques involved invariably disturbed the surrounding rocks; explosives have a massive impact and although the walls and roof of a mine may appear solid and safe, minute cracks will have permeated the rock for a considerable distance. In time, the natural processes of settlement and the sheer weight of rock above may cause a tunnel to weaken and perhaps collapse. If the original tunnel was in any way supported by artificial timber or stone supports this is a clear indication that the passage may be unsound and roof 'break-down' may occur because, over time, the roof supports will have deteriorated.

The movement of air bubbles as they pass through a delicate area of rocks could be sufficient to trigger a collapse. Water is denser than air and helps to support the roof, but when exhausted air accumulates in an unstable region severe destabilisation can occur (a similar problem can occur in wrecks). In many mines roof and wall supports frequently hold back, or conceal, large quantities of loose debris. An underwater collapse at such a site could be catastrophic.

Many old mine workings are therefore inherently dangerous and should be avoided (particularly coal mines), though some disused metal mines – such as iron mines – are relatively stable and these offer excellent prospects for underwater exploration. Each site – indeed, each section of each mine – must be individually and carefully evaluated. Local knowledge is very important.

Apart from considering the type of mine and its stability, the air in abandoned mines is frequently poor and may be depleted of oxygen. While it is seemingly breathable, it may not be capable of sustaining life. There may be an excessive, dangerous accumulation of carbon dioxide or other more lethal gases; methane is explosive, while others might originate from pollution due to irresponsible or unauthorised waste disposal. Remember, therefore, that when surfacing in an 'air' pocket extreme caution must be taken: the gas may not be fit to breathe.

Pollution in mines can be localised or widespread and it frequently affects water quality, which otherwise appears clear, fresh and inviting. However, even the smallest quantity of some pollutants can have a toxic effect.

Abandoned mines may contain fixtures, such as telephone or electrical wiring, pipework and other items left suspended from long bolts driven into the roof and walls, which may also be hazardous. Now discoloured and rusty, in a flooded domain they may be almost invisible and those hanging from above are often not seen until contact is made. If a diver becomes entangled, wire cannot be cut with a knife! Bolts or nails may be sharp enough to cause injury or puncture flotation devices. These factors are equally dangerous in wrecks, where rusting, weakened metalwork may lie in wait for an unwary diver.

Rarely is there a discernible flow in a mine. However, during periods of heavy rainfall quantities of fine silt will invariably be carried underground and produce cloudy water until the sediment settles. Over time these deposits, which also gather upon ledges and fixtures, can present considerable potential for a silt-out. Because the sediment is very fine it is easily disturbed and will rise with the least provocation. Mines are usually complex and maze-like rather than consisting of a single tunnel: to lose visibility and orientation could be fatal.

To sum up, mines must be treated with extreme respect. Just because they offer a convenient access to what seems to be an inviting dive site, remember that rock stability, air and water quality, and abandoned equipment are all potentially hazardous.

Conservation and landowner relationships

The overhead environment presents a very special area of sporting and recreational potential and forms a unique and vulnerable part of our cultural heritage. Caves and mines should be treated with respect: they require careful attention if they are to be conserved for the benefit and enjoyment of future generations. Remember also that wrecks may be registered as a grave or have been granted other protection. Research your mine or wreck dive accordingly, to ensure that your visit is appropriate.

Maintaining the goodwill of landowners is extremely important to ensure future access. Always ask permission to cross land and undertake a dive; involve the owner in the project and supply details of what you find

Everyone venturing into the overhead environment must accept responsibility for practical conservation – we should try to leave a dive site in a better state than that in which we found it. Minimising our impact upon the cave or mine is extremely important. We can all undertake small tasks such as removing an accidentally dropped sweet wrapper or an old, broken line.

However, conservation extends much further than merely 'cleaning up'. All land is owned, either privately or by an organisation, and individuals participating in outdoor and underwater activities must remember to behave responsibly and politely and to leave without argument if requested by a landowner. Conservation demands a close working relationship between divers and landowners, statutory conservation agencies and anyone with a real or perceived interest in this underwater world. Access and environmental matters are becoming increasingly complex and it is only through such partnerships that potential threats to the environment – present or future – can be removed or minimised. Cave and mine entrances are frequently gated and locked, but by demonstrating courtesy and respect access will hopefully be maintained.

Divers are strongly recommended to seek professional advice and undertake appropriate training suitable for the specific overhead environment that interests them. Reading is an aid – caving guidebooks cover all the limestone regions of the British Isles, for example – but, while these are undoubtedly useful, there is no substitute for the information, knowledge and experience that the newcomer will acquire by joining a club or society and meeting others of like mind.

The future well-being of this precious environment lies in our hands; let us do our utmost to protect this realm for those who will follow.

Chapter two
Equipment

THERE is no one specific set of equipment or configuration that can be stipulated or recommended for use in the overhead environment. Each sphere – cave, mine, wreck, ice – differs in its demands and requirements. In general, a good configuration must be completely reliable; through ease of use and comfort it will generate confidence.

Each project should be prepared for and considered thoroughly. The final equipment selection should be governed by a set of general rules:

- Equipment must be appropriate for the area of activity
- Divers should strive to be completely self-reliant, even if working in a team
- The principal of redundancy should apply to all relevant equipment
- Divers should be trained and fully familiar with this equipment before venturing into an overhead environment

Equipment is but a collection of tools; faith in its reliability must never become more important than the art of technique. Safe diving in any overhead environment requires specialised equipment and appropriate technique, not forgetting a structured, gradual acclimatisation.

It follows that divers should maintain an open mind with regard to improving both equipment and techniques, while not dismissing the tried and tested approach that has evolved in each sphere. The equipment configurations adopted in cave diving, for example, are significantly different throughout the world. This is not to say that one approach is better than another, just that local conditions dictate appropriate measures. Wherever you plan to dive you must know your equipment and its limitations.

Self-sufficiency

In an overhead environment divers cannot make an immediate ascent to the surface and it follows that problems must be immediately addressed (and ideally solved) rather than taking what, to an open water diver, would be an obvious course of action: ascend and deal with difficulties at the surface. Cave divers are particularly well versed in problem-solving and it is from this arena that many tried and tested techniques have evolved. All divers should nurture and develop the concept of self-sufficiency. This is not to advocate solo diving, even though in many situations this has proved to be a sound and responsible approach to the overhead environment, but to stress that if you are a competent, self-reliant diver your buddy has less to worry about – and vice versa.

Paul Axton, a former Standards Director overseeing training for the Cave Divers Association of Australia, is wearing a well-configured set of equipment, appropriate for cave diving in the Mount Gambier region of south-east Australia

Reducing stress is all-important and we can prepare for it better than we think we can. It starts with the question: What if?

Novice divers face many potential problems, but training breaks down barriers and provides a framework within which solutions are found.

Cave divers, especially in Europe, have developed and refined solo diving. As a norm they use at least two separate breathing systems: two cylinders, two regulators and two contents gauges. They carry at least three lights (diving lights suited to the overhead environment are discussed further in Chapter 3), two small knives, two dive timers and/or computers plus perhaps a depth gauge, and possibly two masks and two line reels. There will be ample buoyancy and, when necessary, a variety of other equipment is also taken to cover other possible shortcomings, for example a compass (an essential orientation back-up) and submersible 'hard' decompression tables – just in case!

This principle of redundancy, where totally separate systems are carried in case of failure, is taken further when necessary. Redundancy also relates to the air or gas supply, where the diver adheres to the Rule of Thirds: cave divers use only one-third of their air while swimming into the cave, leaving one-third for the outward journey with (in theory) the final third remaining in the cylinder but providing a reserve in case of trouble (air management is discussed further in Chapter 5).

Once you develop this mindset you will become a safer diver.

Dive suits

If the water is cold, you are descending to depth or plan to be immersed for a long period, a drysuit may be essential. However, if you are visiting warmer climes such as the Bahamas or Mexico a thin (3mm or 4mm) wetsuit may be more suitable. For diving deep inside a 'dry' cave system a sensible approach is to wear a thick semi-dry wetsuit.

Prepare according to the nature of the route to the dive base and that of the dive site. Whatever suit you select you must consider its limitations: is there a long walk to reach the water, should you dress at the dive base? What happens if the suit is torn or leaks? Many other questions require attention, but at the outset it is important to address these seemingly minor issues. Forewarned is forearmed. To all intents and purposes water is cold and, as a generalisation, your thermal protection should maintain a stable, comfortable body temperature – before, during and after the dive. Remember: decompression sickness can quickly be induced by overexertion or overheating after a dive, due to the rapid stimulation of blood flow.

When choosing a suit the factors to consider include:

The leading South American diver Gilberto Menezes in a drysuit – essential equipment, even in the tropical caves of the Mato Grosso du Sul, Brazil

- Water temperature
- Planned depth for the dive
- Anticipated dive duration
- Distance and difficulty in reaching the dive site
- Construction and other suit features

For short-duration exploration there is much to commend wearing a good wetsuit. Be it in a cave, mine or shallow wreck, provided buoyancy is correctly calculated at the start of the dive, the fewer complications there are, the better. Having to maintain control of a drysuit which may be prone to gas migration can distract the diver's concentration from other, perhaps more important, essentials.

Depending upon your experience and aptitude a drysuit may be chosen (or be considered essential) from the outset. Carefully consider the type of diving being undertaken, as there are many suits available on the market: some are preferable to others. For the majority of diving in the overhead environment perhaps the most practical and robust suits have a heavy-duty membrane or are made from compressed or crushed neoprene. Manoeuvrability in these suits is better than in those made from 'normal' neoprene, but generally they are not as warm. At depth, neoprene suits will compress and additional thermal protection is therefore required.

A good fit is extremely important; shop around and take your time over this purchase. Experience repeatedly shows that the temptation to purchase a second-hand drysuit, offered at an attractive price, is rarely advantageous in the long term. Sooner or later a 'near-enough' fit will present limitations and a custom-made drysuit is therefore the most cost- and comfort-effective choice. Think carefully about the entry zip position and other features. Across-the-shoulder zips, for example, significantly restrict arm movement, which is important when operating back-mounted cylinder valves. Consider the size of leg pouches, as larger ones increase drag while swimming.

Well-equipped divers preparing to explore the Émergence du Ressel, France

While a drysuit may keep you dry, it might not keep you warm. Consider the worse case scenario: if your suit accidentally floods will you survive the decreased temperature for the duration of decompression? Will you have sufficient buoyancy to surface?

Do not overlook the importance of undergarments in a drysuit. Ensure that your drysuit is not too restricted and can accommodate sufficient thermal protection that will remain warm in case of flooding. Just as in mountain walking, the principal of layering holds good and an effective 'wicking' layer of clothing should be worn next to the skin. A cotton T-shirt is a very poor choice because damp produced by sweating prior to the dive is held next to the skin and will later cause chilling. However, garments made from man-made materials such as Flectalon®, Thinsulate® or wool, plus a thin vest to wick perspiration from the skin will maintain warmth.

A well-fitting drysuit should not cause problems with gas migration, but this can be troublesome in a large suit so be wary of steeply angled, head-first descents. With the change in orientation, air within the drysuit immediately moves from the upper body to the feet and can result in 'ballooning', where the lower part of the suit stretches and the diver's feet are displaced from the boots – causing the loss of fins. Remedying this predicament is not as easy as is supposed. To avoid ballooning, some divers restrict air movement by using Velcro wrap-around 'gaiters' or straps around ankles and/or feet.

Cylinders and configuration

Cylinders of all types and sizes are used in the overhead environment. To pass very short, shallow sumps cave divers may use small, 2 litre cylinders to reach dry areas of cave which are otherwise inaccessible, while long or deep penetrations may require a multiple configuration of 20 litre tanks. Like all parts of the diver's equipment, cylinders require good maintenance; they must be kept in test and handled with care. All manner of cylinders may be effectively adopted provided that the diver has

considered redundancy and general safety.

Cylinders are normally constructed of steel or aluminium, though a small number of activists may adopt carbon fibre composites, particularly for long subterranean missions. While both main types are suitable, steel bottles offer a number of advantages – especially for cave and mine diving – because, considering the pressures involved, they tolerate bumps and scratches better than aluminium. This may not be an important consideration where there is easy access to the dive site, but for diving deep inside a cave or mine steel cylinders are preferred.

A first stage regulator showing an A-clamp attachment (left) equipped with a 'button' pressure gauge, and the more secure DIN regulator attachment (right)

Whatever construction, size, shape or pressure of cylinder you use, it should be protected. Adding mesh is invaluable and a boot may be useful (especially during transport underground), but the valve is the most vulnerable part of a cylinder. Fitting a metal blanking cap over a DIN-fit valve helps to avoid thread damage; if metal caps are unavailable plastic ones will suffice, if only to prevent the penetration of dirt (but note that

Cylinder protection is extremely important in an underground environment. The small, 4 litre cylinder (above) is popular with British cave divers. It is protected with plastic mesh and wrapped with rubber snoopy loops at intervals. Cylinder boots are rarely used; instead, the base is protected with adhesive tape.

The ingenious arrangement of haul sacks, devised by a German team, shows how a system may also form a multi-cylinder backpack for the dive. By using easily detached, quick-fit connections, two of the four cylinders can readily be dropped as stage cylinders during the dive

if a cylinder valve is accidentally opened the cap can become a dangerous projectile; a small hole drilled in the cap minimises this risk). On an awkward underground carry, valves can be protected with foam insulation matting or even an old towel held in place with cord or a rubber snoopy loop.

Redundancy is a key word in the overhead environment and nowhere is this more important than with the air or gas supply. Depending upon your experience and where your initial training is being undertaken, a single cylinder may prove adequate for a short, simple dive. However, the shortcomings of such an approach are obvious. One refinement that has been successfully implemented is to fit a special Y- or H-cylinder valve to connect two independently controlled regulators to the cylinder. This approach has distinct advantages if difficulties ensue.

The limited scope of cavern diving can be accomplished with a single cylinder, but twin cylinders are essential for other overhead environment diving. Size is not necessarily all-important, but both cylinders must be the *same* size, pressure rating and capacity. Ideally, if diving with a companion, you should use the same equipment and configuration – divers with similar configurations are more likely to recognise a partner's equipment problems and will probably be more capable of dealing with an equipment-based emergency.

While redundancy is essential, divers should avoid using a supplementary small 3 litre pony cylinder for anything other than a cavern dive, and here – as in open water – it should only be regarded as an emergency cylinder. A 3 litre cylinder does not provide sufficient air in this environment. To illustrate the point imagine that you are diving solo into a shallow tunnel or passageway, carrying a 12 litre and 3 litre tank. Just before your safe turnaround point (you have used one-third of the air in the large cylinder)

a problem occurs and you are forced to change to your pony set. Given the stress and the distance back to the surface, your increased breathing rate means that it is most unlikely that you will survive. If your main tank capacity was 15 litre you certainly would not return.

Similarly sized cylinders with a pair of regulators are essential for overhead environment diving and there are two configurations of back-mounted twinsets to consider. The first uses two completely independent cylinders, each equipped with a regulator and pressure gauge. The second

These two British divers are training with side-mounted equipment in open water, prior to a cave dive. While redundancy is essential, it is also important not to carry too much equipment

uses a cross-over manifold and is generally regarded as the safest option, especially where access to the water is relatively easy or there is a short carry to the dive site. Where equipment must be transported through difficult underground terrain, perhaps between sumps, it is more practical to adopt a completely independent set-up.

There are several types of manifold arrangements. Those with a single regulator take-off do not equate with the principal of redundancy in the event of a failure. The preferred type – the isolation manifold – has separate cylinder valves and an isolator valve situated midway between the two, meaning that in the event of a failure either regulator may be isolated but the diver can still access all the remaining air. Using a manifold therefore avoids the need to change over mouthpieces during the course of a dive. However, though failures are rare they have been known to occur, even with this system.

Whatever arrangement you opt for it is essential that you can reach all your cylinder

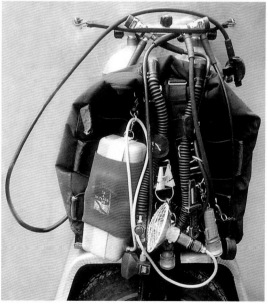

valves – if you cannot operate the isolator there is little point in having one! A solution to this problem is to introduce a 'remote' isolator, basically a hand-operated valve mounted at the end of a length of cable which is conveniently sited beneath an arm. These are affectionately known as 'slob knobs'.

It is important to avoid undue contact with the ever-present ceiling, not only to avoid physical damage to the knobs and manifold, but also to ensure that the supply is not inadvertently closed down. For example,

A comprehensive set of cave diving equipment, attached to the side of a trailer with shock cord, demonstrates a typical configuration used in Florida

Lorraine Hardman about to embark on a dive in Tank Cave, the most extensive and complex underwater network in Australia. Her equipment is neatly stowed and thoroughly streamlined

because the valves face in different directions, rubbing the right-hand valve while swimming forwards has no effect because this is the 'on' direction – but rubbing the left-hand valve will turn it off. Given the vulnerable position of cylinder valves, it is also strongly advised that DIN fittings are used for maximum security as they are less likely to loosen if knocked.

Damage to cylinder valves, the manifold or vulnerable hose take-offs must be avoided. However, contact with the ceiling will occur on occasion and valve guards or cages have been developed for precisely this reason, although the subject is one of heated debate. Divers opposed to this form of security may cite poor technique (buoyancy control), undue speed and a lack of general awareness. However, many of the world's leading activists chose to incorporate this level of protection in their rig and no one doubts their level of competence. Hopefully, all will agree that good technique and caution are extremely important.

No matter what configuration of cylinders is adopted it is important to breathe air evenly between the two. It is therefore crucial that pre-dive safety checks are thorough to ensure that the isolator valve is open and both cylinders are full; there have been instances where the centre valve was closed when filling took place, leaving one cylinder empty. Some divers prefer to check the cylinder contents and then turn the isolator valve until it is almost closed, so that if a problem arises during the dive a much faster shut-down is possible. However, under stress there is the danger of turning the valve in the wrong direction, wasting rather than saving time. Some manifold designs require that the isolator is fully open during use, which will take longer to isolate the site of the failure.

If the diver uses two separate breathing systems (independent singles) it is important to change mouthpieces on a regular basis, for example every five minutes. This means that pressure gauges are frequently monitored, a very good habit, and – apart from maintaining good trim as the cylinders empty evenly – it also generates confidence in the 'spare' mouthpiece, as you know that it was working perfectly only a few minutes before.

There is a lot to be said for keeping a firm hold of that life-sustaining regulator, but exchanging one for another is not as difficult or threatening as some divers might perceive. Providing that both regulators are well maintained and positioned conveniently to enable a quick and efficient changeover, this exercise is a tremendous confidence builder. It is, in effect, your 'silent buddy' right there with you – instantly accessible and totally dependable.

Regulators and hoses

There should be no compromise on safety with regard to regulators: buy the best. There are numerous high quality regulators on the market, but before you part with money seek the final word from someone you trust and respect who regularly dives in the overhead environment. Remember that you will need to undertake basic maintenance on the regulator –

the more you know about your kit and its limitations the better – and that it will require periodic, comprehensive servicing by a fully trained and competent person. Not all service engineers have the same quality of workmanship and dive technicians hold your life in their hands. Test your kit somewhere safe after a service or lay-off.

Considerable care in hose choice and routing is required regardless of whether you use back- or side-mounted cylinders. Hoses should lie in a tidy manner close to the body so that the potential for them to catch on things is low. Streamlining is the operative word; there is nothing worse than a configuration where hoses protrude from all sides of the first stage, looking like a Christmas tree.

Hoses should be of optimum length and rigged to allow fast, efficient deployment. With a dual outlet manifold system a pressure gauge on a standard, long hose is often attached to only one first stage – generally the back-up regulator –

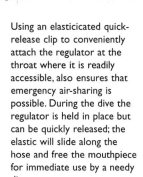

Using an elasticated quick-release clip to conveniently attach the regulator at the throat where it is readily accessible, also ensures that emergency air-sharing is possible. During the dive the regulator is held in place but can be quickly released; the elastic will slide along the hose and free the mouthpiece for immediate use by a needy diver

while the buoyancy compensator inflation hose is attached to the other. If diving with back-mounted independent cylinders each regulator is equipped with a pressure gauge, while in a dual compensator system (for example, a pair of wings or a single wing and a drysuit) inflator connections are made with separate first stages. This means that if a regulator fails the ability to inflate a buoyancy device is retained. Likewise, dual connectors should be identical and therefore interchangeable in the event of failure.

The hose configuration depends in part on the system: back-mounted or side-mounted cylinders. Most regulators have hoses which feed from the right-hand side. In a back-mounted system, therefore, both can pass over the right shoulder to lie in the correct position at the neck, conveniently accessible for regulator swap-overs. However, in a side-mounted arrangement the left-hand cylinder should feed to the regulator from the left of the body, which requires a non-handed design such as the Poseidon that allows the hose to be fed from either side of the body with the regulator remaining in the correct orientation at the neck.

Even in a back-mounted system, for absolute clarity as to which valve is connected to which cylinder, it is better to feed the hose from the left-hand cylinder over the left shoulder. For any configuration, colour-code regulators using electrical insulation tape to match their contents gauge and perhaps the neck strap – a cheap and effective system.

Close attention must be paid to the way that regulators hang at the neck. When making a swap-over, or in an emergency, time is critical and removing one from your mouth and replacing it with the other must be accomplished in a matter of seconds. Neck straps made from surgical

Side-mounting cylinders is becoming increasingly common worldwide. This American equipment configuration, manufactured by Dive Rite, enables the diver to pass low constrictions more easily than if a back-mounted configuration was used

tubing are commonly used by technical divers, but a system of elasticated quick-release plastic fastenings is also very effective. This allows for fast, easy and complete regulator detachment from the normal position close to the throat, for air-sharing with a buddy. A team of divers working together on a regular basis should standardise their rigging even down to this level.

Air-sharing is a prime consideration. Adhering to the safe limitations of cavern diving, a normal octopus regulator might be used to provide essential redundancy in an emergency – but an octopus does not confer true redundancy because both regulators share the same first stage and air supply. In addition, standard length octopus hoses, and the fact that most regulators are designed to enter the mouth from the right-hand side, are limiting. Problems are frequently discovered when divers sharing air try to establish a reasonable swimming position, which adds to stress in an already stressful situation.

This is where a 1.5m or 2m hose is highly advantageous. However, it is impractical to quickly 'pass-off' or unwind a

A side-mount configuration can be based on a steel back-plate, but the system will be more difficult to carry to distant underground sites, especially in restricted environments

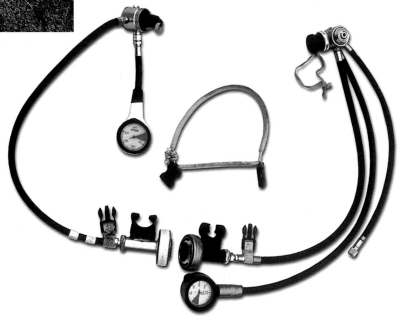

The first and second stage elements of a side-mount configuration. Non-handed regulators can be fed from either side of the body, which is extremely advantageous on the left-hand side where a right-handed regulator will not readily lie in the optimum position.

There are different methods for attaching the regulators so that they are ready for use at the front of the neck, with the primary requirement that they are instantly accessible. This arrangement uses a neck loop (pictured in the centre) with two quick-release clips which snap into those on each regulator

2m hose from around the neck if a helmet with torches is worn; in an emergency there is every likelihood that the helmet and, in all probability, the mask will be displaced. If a helmet is worn the long hose should be deployed elsewhere, perhaps stored along the length of the cylinder where it is tucked beneath snoopy loops or elastic shock cord. Ensure that it cannot catch on other items of equipment when it is pulled free. Always think carefully: 'What happens if . . .'

Using a short hose attachment to each pressure gauge is strongly advocated with side-mounted cylinders, although conventional long high pressure hoses can easily be deployed along the length of the cylinder by stowing the excess beneath bungee or snoopy loops. 'Small and neat' is important in the overhead environment and with this in mind it is also advisable to avoid large consoles.

With such streamlining comes the philosophy of simplicity, affectionately referred to as KISS: Keep It Simple, Stupid. Part and parcel of this is an attempt to reduce the number of potential failure points in the system. An example based on practical decompression equipment illustrates this point well. Where oxygen content is high, as here, it is desirable to have as short a length of high pressure hose as possible to minimise the risk of failure – and there is frequently no high pressure hose at all (instead, divers monitor the gas with a small 'button' gauge attached directly to the first stage).

Weighting

Open water divers are taught that a weight belt is the last item of equipment to be put on before entering the water and the first piece of equipment to be dropped in an emergency. While this is excellent instruction for a novice heading for the surface in open water, it is not true in the overhead environment. Being pinned against the roof by positive buoyancy can be as disastrous as being overly heavy at depth.

Most cave divers build their basic weight requirement into their harness, or bolt V-weights beneath the back-plate, so that there is no chance of accidentally dropping weights. It is worth noting that the waist is not necessarily the best place to locate lead as there is every likelihood that a stationary diver will then assume a feet down, head up position in the water. Even if this is not the case the diver's orientation will tend towards this state, and when moving off the diver will disturb light sediment lying on the floor. Maintaining the body in a predominantly horizontal attitude – a level trim (see p81) – is very important because the diver should then be able to fin with a minimal disturbance to sediment. Retaining visibility, to the best of one's ability, is extremely important and the position of lead on the body has a considerable impact.

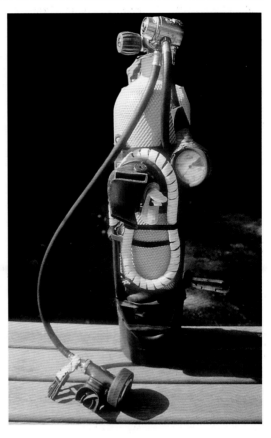

A spare regulator, with a long hose for air-sharing, may be incorporated into side-mount configurations. The hose is retained under shock cord or rubber snoopy loops. Positioning is important to ensure that the regulator is protected, yet instantly removable in an emergency

Buoyancy compensators and harnesses

Other than on the shortest and shallowest of dives, divers must control and regulate their buoyancy. Indeed, wearing two cylinders (plus the rest of the accoutrements) makes it likely that weighting will vary by several kilograms during the course of a dive, because as air is used up this decreases the weight carried and when weight decreases, buoyancy increases. To counteract this effect sufficient lead has to be carried at the start of the dive, in anticipation of needs at the end. The diver therefore carries the greatest weight at the start of the dive.

The subject needs careful consideration as there are several variables to take into account. Much depends upon the precise diving environment, the suit you chose to wear and the size and type of the cylinders. All divers should address and evaluate buoyancy changes by experimenting in safe water while using both full and nearly empty cylinders with appropriate weights, before entering the overhead environment. The onset of positive buoyancy, perhaps within the last (emergency) third of the air supply, might be critical.

Changes in weight during the dive are controlled using a buoyancy

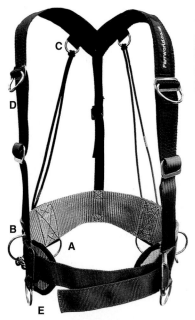

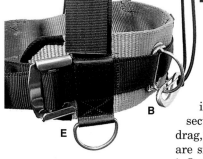

Explorer harness

The Explorer I harness is based on the American side-mount system, commonly used in the UK, where the bottoms of the cylinders are fastened to stainless steel D-rings (either A or B, the latter being moveable around the waist). Bungee cord runs from (C), which is also used to fix a wing; this clips to (B) while the harness is put on, then moved under the arm to (D).

The diver in (1) has attached a cylinder to D-ring (B) on his left-hand side; it is then swung upright to lie alongside the body (2). With the cylinder correctly positioned the bungee cord is twisted around the cylinder valve to hold it in place against the body (3), before being clipped to (D).

Dive reels may be attached to the lower D-ring (E)

compensator (BC). It is generally accepted that the primary compensator should provide at least 25kg of lift, to ensure that a diver can regain the surface at the start of a dive. Some divers use dual buoyancy compensators, creating a considerably greater capacity for control. This may be reassuring in open water, but in an overhead environment this apparent security raises its own concerns. A bulky compensator increases drag, resulting in higher energy expenditure. Ironically, many divers are significantly overweighted, which requires that they partially inflate their buoyancy – thus exacerbating the problem.

A set of wings is the favoured buoyancy system for a back-mounted configuration. Wings comprise a U-shaped bladder which produces buoyancy at your back, sandwiched between you and your cylinders. As such the entire rig is comfortable and streamlined, requiring a minimum of strapping, encumbrance and chest compression. This is an important consideration with a dry suit, as you need easy access to the inflation valve(s).

There are two types of wing: bondage and non-bondage. The former has loops of shock cord set around the bladder, while the second does not and presents a much simpler, flatter profile. Each has advantages and disadvantages. A bondage wing stays close to the body at all times, while a flat, non-bondage wing is prone to flapping and this possibly increases drag. Elasticated loops can be used to restrict air movement within the wing's bladder, but this added pressure means that air is vented rapidly when the dump valve is operated. Environmental considerations are also extremely important when making your choice of wing: elasticated loops, for example, are prone to catch on rocks or protuberances in a restricted cave passage or wreck, and here a small, flat wing is preferable. Buoyancy redundancy must be considered carefully, especially if the diver is not wearing a drysuit (with its own capacity for buoyancy). For deeper dives, certainly greater than 30m, redundancy is essential.

Jackets or vests can also be employed to good advantage. Where the environment is confined and the diver is using a side-mounted configuration, it is comforting to have all the equipment snugly wrapped around the body. In this situation a dual bag construction BC is strongly recommended to avoid accidental damage. A potential disadvantage with a jacket arrangement lies in the quantity of clutter about the chest and the possibility that a well-inflated bag may create breathing difficulties due to chest compression. However, as with any system, familiarity and critical evaluation are the keys to successful operation and an increased safety margin.

Remember: if you use two forms of buoyancy control they must take their supply from separate regulators. Small capacity pony bottles have limited purpose in this respect. In terms of neatness or cleanliness, note that the inflate–deflate corrugated hose on most buoyancy compensators is too long and may therefore be difficult to streamline. Consider refitting the BC with a shorter hose, perhaps coupled with a shorter inflator. It must be stressed that the diver should strive to establish the correct balance between the BC, cylinders, weighting and suit.

No one harness is perfect for all overhead environments. For example, side-mounting harnesses are very different from those used for conventional back-mounting applications. Some harnesses claim to be sufficiently versatile to be used for both back- and side-mounts, but some features are inevitably compromised in the design. The environment is the key: choose your harness accordingly.

This popular American-designed Halcyon harness and non-bondage wing shows how back-up lights can be attached. While the harness is excellent for use in warm water, it is not ideal in every environment. Activating the pull-cord to the secondary, lower air dump valve might prove impossible in some situations, such as in cold water when thick gloves are worn

Some divers insist that back-mounted cylinders are best carried on a plate and threaded with a continuous, single length of webbing. Here, the size of the padded shoulder loops is fixed and final adjustments take place at the waist when the set is put on. This may offer sufficient control underwater, but where entry (and, more precisely, exit) from the water is difficult it is frequently better to incorporate a single adjustable shoulder release. Quick-release plastic buckles may be controversial, but the ability to get out of a harness quickly while possibly alone in difficult conditions is an important consideration.

Stage cylinders

In the majority of overhead environments, especially the popular cave diving areas of the world, it is common to carry a third set of breathing apparatus. This technique is known as staging. The set may be required for decompression or to facilitate long penetrations into cave systems, and the cylinders can be dropped off for later use wherever the dive plan dictates or breathed for a distance along the route before being set aside until the return.

Such advanced techniques require that great care and attention is given to the added complications that arise. Cave divers, for example, should not embark upon this progression until they are completely comfortable and experienced with their basic equipment and its configuration. This

Stage cylinders used in Florida or Mexico are generally attached to the diver using bolt-snap connectors. The connection may be varied slightly, according to where the diver requires the stage cylinder to lie in the water. The right-hand photograph shows cylinders rigged for use in a low, constricted network of passages

Carrying a stage cylinder

A popular UK technique for carrying a front-mounted stage cylinder is to use a simple harness made from shock cord. The cylinder is slipped under the cord and supported at two points on the front of the body.

A karabiner placed on the upper cord makes the system easier to put on, but its main purpose is to enable the diver to locate it during the dive, perhaps when hands are cold and visibility is poor; for the same reason, a bolt-snap is placed on the waist cord. For clarity, the regulator has not been attached to the cylinder in these photographs

shock cord

support points

text only touches on the subject of staging, noting that apart from increasing a diver's range of activity from the dive base the technique can also generate a greater safety margin by increasing redundancy.

Stage cylinders should be as close to neutrally buoyant as possible; do not use excessively heavy or buoyant bottles. Aluminium cylinders with a capacity of 10 or 11 litres are preferred, while 300 bar steel cylinders should be avoided as these are negatively buoyant even when empty. Consider also that, like every other item of your equipment, the regulator fitted to this stage cylinder must be totally reliable; do not use a cheap or poorly maintained 'spare' regulator. Finally, it is a good idea to use similar DIN-fit valves on your main cylinders and stage bottles, so that they can be exchanged should the need arise.

Stage cylinders are positioned, carried and used in a variety of ways dependent upon the environment. They may be back-mounted as part of a fixed rig, side- or front-mounted, or carried under one arm for a short distance – instantly ready to be dropped off. Rigging for ease of attachment and detachment is a must (otherwise you will waste time and gas). Colour-coding regulators and contents gauges is essential, while hose containment and streamlining requires careful consideration. During more advanced operations where different gas mixtures are used, a diver should be able to identify each cylinder and the gas it contains by feel, for example by using a different type of regulator. In a silt-out this might prove a lifesaver. On complex and committing penetrations, in Florida for example, some divers may complete most if not the entire dive while breathing from stage bottles, retaining back-mount cylinders in reserve and allowing a much simpler, uncluttered exit in an emergency.

Using bolt-snap connectors to attach stage cylinders is probably the most common approach, certainly in reasonably warm water. Some cave divers, operating in cold water, adopt the simple technique of carrying a bottle against their stomach and chest using a pair of elastic loops stretched around the diver's body. The cylinder requires no dressing, apart from a couple of rubber snoopy loops set around its mid-section to contain the hoses leading to the regulator and pressure gauge. The 'stage' is attached by pushing the base of the cylinder into the waist-mounted elastic loop, then inserting the cylinder valve, with regulator attached, beneath the chest-mounted elastic. It takes literally seconds to remove or replace cylinders using this simple rig.

You must also be able to locate and recover the cylinder en route out of the cave, in perhaps greatly reduced visibility. Anticipating this, the 'stage' must be positioned with care when dropped off; the valve on the bottle should be closed to ensure there is no accidental loss of gas, but the regulator must be left pressurised; this retains air for immediate use and prevents water from reaching the first stage. Depending upon the environment consider placing the regulator mouthpiece inside a thin polythene bag to avoid it being contaminated with foreign matter. On the outward dive, or in the event of an emergency, this flimsy bag can be quickly torn aside with very little effort (ensure that the bag remains attached to the hose so that it is not left behind to pollute the cave).

Line reels

The role of the line, carried on a reel (discussed further in Chapter 4), cannot be overemphasised. Reels are specialised items which vary in size and type according to purpose, design and thickness of line (as well as, possibly, the line's markings or labels). Terms such as primary, safety and gap (or jump) are often used to describe a reel's function.

Primary reels – often referred to as penetration reels – generally contain between 50m and 150m of line and are most commonly used to run a guideline from the surface to the start of a permanent cave line, which is situated some distance from the entrance. Larger versions may be used for original exploration; a primary reel might also be used to enter a wreck. Gap or jump reels are smaller, with perhaps 20m to 30m of line, and are used to join the main line or lines to others situated at the side of the passage in a complex system – they are therefore used to bridge a gap between established *in situ* lines.

Safety reels are carried in case of emergency, perhaps line loss or breakage. The amount of line on the reel depends entirely upon the environment, but is generally a minimum of 30m in warm, clear conditions with

Front-mounted stage units are commonly used by British cave divers. Given the amount of equipment held on or close to the diver's chest, regulators, gauges and hoses should be conspicuously colour-coded to avoid confusion when visibility is poor

10m being adequate in cold, murky water. Smaller, more basic line holders are known as finger spools.

Other equipment

Experience and streamlining require that overhead environment divers do not use a snorkel. Underwater in a cave, mine or wreck using a snorkel is wholly inappropriate and it may entangle in the line. A snorkel might be used during a surface approach to a cavern or wreck, but should be removed before entry.

As noted at the start of this chapter, overhead environment divers must strive for self-sufficiency and complete redundancy and all eventualities must be considered and planned for, certainly by a solo diver. Try to carry two of everything: two reels, two knives, two dive timers or computers, and perhaps even two masks. Check all straps for damage before use.

In the overhead environment masks should be low profile and preferably low volume. Accidental displacement must be avoided at all costs. With a snugly-fitting helmet the chances are that a mask will not be displaced or damaged, but if this should occur it is reassuring to know that you can overcome the problem. Knives should be compact with a short blade and, for accessibility, worn either on the arm or upper body. They should not be worn on the leg.

Examples of two types of fin. The traditional jet fin, used by technical divers for many years, is on the right. The larger split fin on the left is a more recent innovation that is becoming increasingly popular due its comparatively light weight and the thrust it develops in use

Fins must be appropriate for the task and the shorter 'jet fin' has a lot to commend it, particularly where there is fine silt. Longer fins such as those adopted by free-divers have little place in the overhead environment, but split fins have proved to be highly energy efficient and can be used to great advantage. It is obvious that fins must remain on the feet, so quick-release fastenings and fragile clips are best avoided. Whatever fin retainers or heel strap arrangements are used, ensure that buckles are well covered. As with the mask strap, tape down any loose ends. Another approach is to use a 10cm wide loop of car inner tube which, after the diver's foot has been inserted, can be slid towards the ankle to cover the entire buckle. Chosen carefully for a snug fit, this little 'extra' can be left permanently on the shoe section of the fin; it will ensure that your fin strap never catches in the line and that the attachment cannot come undone. As with the mask and other straps, periodically check fin straps for signs of deterioration.

Complete redundancy adds a lot of arm-mounted instrumentation which can become a distraction if it works loose; this possibility should be eliminated. Consider replacing the buckle, or perhaps the entire instrument strap, with a loop of 2cm to 5cm wide elastic, which will grip an arm better than a thick rubber strap. Elasticated straps are effective at all depths, will hold equally perfectly on a 3mm wetsuit or a thick drysuit, are much faster to attach than any buckle-based system, and are easy to reposition underwater – even one-handed.

Keep like instruments together. If something fails, or is producing a doubtful reading, you do not want to fumble in a BC pocket (or anywhere else) to locate the back-up – you need a quick and easy comparison between instruments. This is especially important with computers. Continuously monitoring depth and decompression status is essential, but carefully consider redundancy. If you do not have two computers on the dive carry a set of submersible 'hard' decompression tables (and know

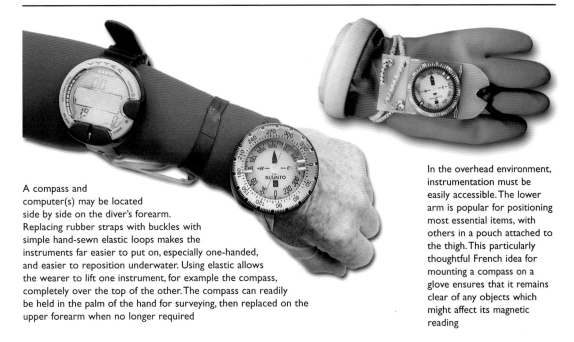

A compass and computer(s) may be located side by side on the diver's forearm. Replacing rubber straps with buckles with simple hand-sewn elastic loops makes the instruments far easier to put on, especially one-handed, and easier to reposition underwater. Using elastic allows the wearer to lift one instrument, for example the compass, completely over the top of the other. The compass can readily be held in the palm of the hand for surveying, then replaced on the upper forearm when no longer required

In the overhead environment, instrumentation must be easily accessible. The lower arm is popular for positioning most essential items, with others in a pouch attached to the thigh. This particularly thoughtful French idea for mounting a compass on a glove ensures that it remains clear of any objects which might affect its magnetic reading

how to use them!).

With just a little thought it is easy to position your two knives side by side or back to back, remembering to mount your compass on the other arm, well away from any metal which could affect its reading. The dive line is your lifeline to the surface, but do not underestimate the importance of a compass. With training, experience and confidence, this tool can be a lifesaver; it should be regarded as an essential back-up to diver orientation.

Dive slates may be categorised according to purpose: decompression and communication. As with all equipment used in the overhead environment, slates must be compact and readily accessible. Slates can be made of plastic or waterproof paper. Always carry two pencils, preferably attached to the communication slate.

Items intended to be stowed in a pocket must be considered carefully. Such items include line arrows or clothes pegs/pins, which are attached to the guideline to indicate the outward direction. Perhaps carried on a length of surgical tubing, it is important that nothing floats loosely so that it might escape and be lost. It is essential that the contents of the pocket are, therefore, attached in some way – perhaps to a grommet in the pouch itself. There is then no danger of losing something when the pocket is opened.

José de Veer wearing an equipment configuration typical of the Belgian and Netherlands region of Europe

This knife, fitted with an elastic wrist strap, is an ideal cutting tool. The blade is easily retractable, even while wearing thick gloves, and it will last many months before needing replacement (though it will corrode faster in salt water than fresh water). Position the knife where it is readily accessible, beneath the wide, elastic straps of a normal diving knife

Equipment selection for this demanding environment must be made carefully. Just as tools must be readily locatable for routine maintenance, so too must you be able to find things when they are needed underwater. This is essential in times of stress. Various strategies may be employed to fine-tune your equipment configuration, and thinking of all the hazards or things that might go wrong during a particular dive is an important first step. Sit in the privacy of your home, in your kit, and address each scenario in turn. This exercise frequently reveals inadequacies in the configuration, perhaps highlighting basic omissions or possibly items you do not need.

No discussion of equipment is complete without a brief comment about the condition of the diver's body and mind, which is of paramount importance. Individuals should carefully consider their level of health and fitness, and structure activities in a responsible manner. Unfit people can certainly dive, but it is clear that their ability to manage exertion and stress (see Chapter 7) will be compromised.

A knife attached to the forearm using elastic straps is quick and easy to put on. The risk of losing the knife when it is withdrawn is eliminated by first inserting a hand through its attached snoopy loop, before it is taken from its sheath

Equipment

- Choose your equipment carefully and stick with it; use equipment regularly to develop trust and confidence in it
- New equipment requires careful induction; regularly check older kit
- Equipment must be thoroughly reliable, fit for the purpose, streamlined and comfortable to wear
- Understand your equipment and be able to instantly reach it
- Maximum efficiency in a team is achieved when all members have directly comparable equipment and adopt the same configurations and systems
- Look after your equipment and your equipment will look after you!

Chapter three
Lights

AN analysis of fatalities that have occurred in the overhead environment over the past thirty years clearly shows that lighting has been an important contributory factor. Perhaps we have become complacent – yet in the overhead environment we are totally dependent on lights and these, of all the ancillary equipment used by divers, remain the items most prone to failure.

It is clear that a light is required in the dark, but the subject is more complex than it may first appear. Ironically, it is a sad fact that untrained individuals are more likely to be lured 'just a little further' into the overhead environment if they are carrying a light, than if they are not. This is understandable, but also dangerous.

Ambient light levels near an entrance can, and do, fall dramatically if silt is disturbed. Once this occurs neither the daylight outside nor the diver's own light is of much use. The scenario has been observed in numerous cases in the caves of Florida and the Bahamas where, tragically, if the diver has no guideline the outcome has frequently been fatal. That a diver with a light is drawn more readily into a cave has led to the implementation of a 'no lights' rule at a growing number of commercial and national park cave diving sites in the USA, removing any spontaneous temptation. This is better than totally banning uncertified open water divers, though the policy can only be effective if the site is well supervised.

It is essential that divers entering the overhead environment carry reliable lighting to contend with the darkness. For a basic cavern dive, or short penetrations into wrecks under good levels of ambient light, divers should carry at least two independent forms of lighting (all training agencies stress that the primary illumination is daylight at a cavern level of certification, thus meaning that there are three light sources available).

Head-mounted lighting is normal for cave and mine exploration in the UK. This diver is equipped with a variety of lights, including a main helmet light with both a halogen bulb and LEDs (producing a powerful beam as well as a long-duration light), and a more powerful hand-held high intensity discharge (HID) system

For cave or mine penetration – the realm of permanent, total darkness – the minimum is three separate lights, and it is common for cave divers in the UK and Europe to carry many more. The reason is simple: redundancy.

The most important factors to consider when choosing a light are 'burn time' (ideally, all lights should last for at least one and a half times the duration of the anticipated dive; the main light, or primary, should last for twice the dive duration) and output (how much illumination is generated). It is worth stating emphatically that lights are only as good as the batteries they contain and it is strongly recommended that different types of batteries are used in different units. The prudent diver uses a mixture of alkaline and rechargeable batteries to avoid potential embarrassment; number batteries and use them in sets. Ensure you know the expected duration of each light unit with the batteries it holds and, if back-up lights contain disposable batteries, serious thought must be given to when

and how often they are replaced.

All lights may fail due to problems with batteries, bulbs or, as happens occasionally, a leaking O-ring seal. Batteries may be partly used or not fully charged – regularly check both batteries and the charger for correct output. Always carry one or two switched-off safety or back-up lights containing new or fully charged batteries for emergency use. The type and rating of the bulb affects both the duration and brightness of a light and a change of bulb may radically affect the burn time. Light and battery technologies are constantly advancing and, as with any other item of equipment, divers should keep abreast of new developments; for example, some compact head-mounted LED lights will last well over 25 hours.

Lighting is employed differently around the world. By far the majority of cave divers, for example in Florida and Mexico, use powerful hand-held units as primary lights. While they are designed to be hand-held, it is extremely important to ensure that holding the light does not preclude the diver from undertaking other functions. Rather than a pistol grip, which involves holding the unit in the palm of the hand, a Goodman-style holder is strongly recommended. In this system the diver slips four fingers through the handle frame (which may be rigid and metallic, or made from elasticated shock cord), placing the light head on the back of the hand and leaving fingers and thumb free to perform other tasks. The light head is powered by a battery pack, mounted appropriately.

In the technical diving community light heads (the reflector and bulb, powered via a cable leading to a battery) are normally mounted on a rigid, Goodman-style handle, which places the light on the back of the hand and allows the diver the continued use of fingers (top). The handle is generally equipped with a bolt-snap, to attach the unit to the diver's harness while not in use – this is also a convenient place to carry plastic line markers.

Rubber tubing on a traditional light forms a cheap but highly effective alternative to a Goodman-style handle

Good illumination goes a long way towards reducing the intimidation of darkness, though it is only when a main light is extinguished and a back-up is used instead that its true psychological support can be gauged. Divers are capable of safely following lines in conditions of poor lighting (2 watt), but when a 50 watt halogen bulb or a 10 watt xenon arc high intensity discharge (HID) system is used you can see much more and the difference between a shallow alcove in the wall and a side tunnel leading to the unknown becomes clear. Good lighting provides a more complete picture of the environment – and the more complete the picture, the more relaxed the diver.

The position of the light is important. Light is scattered by suspended particles in water – the same effect is seen when car headlights are used at full beam in fog and visibility is lost when the light is reflected directly back to the user. A helmet-mounted light may create the same difficulty, but moving the source away from the eyes by hand-holding the primary light largely avoids the problem. A hand-held light is also easily aimed – an important factor because it is important not to dazzle your companions when diving as part of a team .

If a helmet is not used to carry spare lights, these must be readily available from easily retrievable positions. Small neoprene sleeves, or loops of elastic, are invaluable as they can snugly hold virtually any item, but still permit rapid access. Stowing spare lights on the harness, below the level of the shoulder, is preferred as they are easy to locate and remove. Do not clip lights to an attachment and leave them to dangle.

In Britain, cave divers normally carry lights on their helmets. Dazzling companions is less crucial as most dives are conducted solo. The major advantages are that hands are completely free and that, no matter which way the head is turned, the environment in front of the diver is illuminated. In addition the entire array of arm-mounted instrumentation can be read at a glance, which may not be easy using a hand-held light.

Perhaps the most globally popular lights used for both helmet mounting and as a back-up are those powered by three C-cells. Longer (or more bulky) units are cumbersome and, especially in low tunnels, get in the way. It is not uncommon for European cave divers to carry five or more lights on a routine dive, of which it is essential that at least one has a long duration – especially underground where there may be a long haul to reach the dive base where lengthy kitting up takes place.

A small back-up light can be attached to a helmet using elastic. Lights mounted on helmets are often paired, optimally placed low on each side to aid streamlining and helping to avoid catching on rocks

For protracted operations in caves and mines most divers adopt a main light which is reliably expected to last for ten or twenty hours. Long-duration, sealed nickel cadmium (nicad) or nickel metal hydride (Ni-MH) lights are manufactured for the caving market and are more compact, robust and inexpensive compared with those specifically developed for the diving market. When used underwater the headpiece may leak at depth but, nevertheless, such lights have proved invaluable to British cave divers at freshwater sites, though they should not be used in salt water. The traditional miners' lead-acid light, as occasionally used by cavers, should *never* be used in either fresh or salt water.

Given the physical constraints on the size of lights that are conferred by cave and mine environments, and the need for a long burn time, these lights tend to have limited output (a maximum of 6 watts or 10 watts) compared with the high wattage units favoured by divers at sites where access to water is relatively easy.

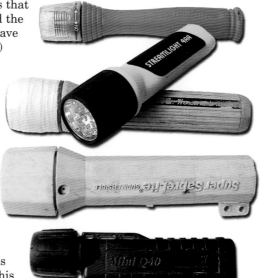

Cave divers in the Americas are trained to use lighting to its best effect. Attracting a buddy's attention is relatively simple with a powerful light, but if the team's lights are dissimilar it is possible that a diver with a weaker unit will not be able to catch the attention of the diver ahead: the weaker beam is overpowered by the lead diver's stronger light. This could be critical in a sudden crisis; the problem may be avoided by ensuring that the lead diver always carries the weakest light. However, it is normal that the lead diver becomes the last one to exit when the divers turn around, but this places the weaker light once more at the back. In this scenario the divers should change places so that the diver with the weaker beam leads out; by maintaining the dive order everyone knows where everyone else is. If a primary light fails the dive would normally be turned, in which case the diver with the failed light (now using a reserve) should either lead or (preferably) be positioned in the middle of a group. For obvious reasons, a diver using a reserve light should not be left to take up the rear.

Examples of torches suitable for helmet-mounting or back-up lights, perhaps carried in a pouch

Underwater communication is often difficult as it relies almost entirely on sight, which is affected by water clarity and lighting. Lighting can be invaluable for attracting attention, though great care must be taken not

A robust back-up light with a bolt-snap connector (above) for clipping to a conventional harness strap. Avoid it dangling by also slipping the light into a short length of neoprene sleeve attached to the harness, which streamlines the arrangement (see p33, where two lights are attached to a Halcyon harness).

With the advantage of longer burn times, HID lighting (right) is not only highly effective, but also significantly reduces the size of battery packs compared with traditional halogen-powered units

to shine lights directly into a diver's eyes; the effects are short-lived but are nevertheless a nuisance as it may take over a minute to regain satisfactory vision. When using head-mounted lights avoid direct eye contact so that you do not dazzle your companion; instead, communicate by shining light on an outstretched limb and use hand signals (see p78). Alternatively, if your buddy is close enough, reflect light to your face so that it can be seen. Facial expressions perhaps produce the ultimate in communication, though this is not always viable. However, if your buddy system is efficient you can gauge how your companion is faring using other observations – avoid dazzle, but pay regular attention to and monitor the activities of your companion.

Rapidly flashing a light, either by repeatedly covering it or by side-to-side arm movement, quickly communicates 'trouble'. However, do not turn the main control switch rapidly on and off as this often causes bulb failure. Crucially, HID lighting takes almost a minute to attain full brightness and, when turned on ('struck') it should remain lit for five minutes before being turned off. If it is quickly turned on and off, carbon deposits from incomplete combustion accumulate in the bulb and its life is greatly shortened – an important point considering the high price of these bulbs.

Lights

- Carry at least three battery powered lights (for cavern diving the primary light is the sun)
- The primary light should last for at least twice the planned dive time
- Keep at least one light turned off, for use in an emergency
- A minimum of one light should be powered by non-rechargeable batteries
- For team diving, primary lights should be matched to each other
- Other than a Goodman-handle light, securely attach lights to a helmet or via short clips or sleeves to the diver's body; do not use lanyards
- Ensure that all batteries are fully charged prior to the dive – avoid complacency!

Chapter four
Guidelines

WHETHER exploring beneath ice, penetrating the dark and gloomy confines of a wreck or swimming through the majestic galleries of a flooded cave, a diver *must* use a continuous guideline connected to the point of entry or dive base. A physical connection between the diver and the line is not recommended; in some situations a karabiner snapped on the line and connected to the diver's wrist could prove hazardous.

Direct sight (or touch, in the case of nil visibility) of the line is essential; the diver should preferably swim directly adjacent to it so that, should visibility decrease or a silt-out occur, the line can be held and the diver can continue safely. Analysing incidents shows that the primary factor in the majority of overhead environment fatalities, other than deficient training, has been the lack (or loss) of the guideline.

The late Sheck Exley, a pioneer of accident analysis, cites the following example in his book *Basic Cave Diving* to illustrate the importance of using a line. On 7 May 1978 two young sailors arrived at Royal Springs in Florida. Neither had any training in scuba or cave diving. They entered the spring, notorious for its deep mud, without a line; one did not have either a light or a pressure gauge. When they failed to resurface cave divers were alerted and they duly recovered both bodies. The one without the light was found at a depth of 9m approximately 50m from the entrance, while the second was located about 68m further into the system. Both had exhausted their air supplies.

The incident began as a catalogue of potential disasters, but it is clear that depth was not a factor. Yet, even without a light and perhaps while low on air, the pair could conceivably have made their exit – had they known which way to go; without a guideline they were doomed. Sadly, a father and son made a similar mistake in the same cave in February 2001 when, without specific training or a line, they disturbed the silt and ran out of air.

A guideline is preferably laid from above the water surface (or from a position at shallow depth that has air directly above); it must be continuous with no breaks or gaps. You might be forced to make an exit from a tunnel in a complete blackout due to a silt-out, light failure or simply the dark of night on the surface and the line position should take this possibility into account. To the uninitiated diver one underwater tunnel may appear much like another, especially when silt obscures visibility. Loss of orientation is extremely stressful and, at the very least, it will cause the diver to breathe more air.

While it is possible for line to be paid out to a diver underwater by someone on dry land (perhaps inside a cave while a diver tackles a constricted sump), or by a diver to a buddy tentatively probing the inside of a wreck, the technique is very limiting. A base-fed line is most successfully used for ice diving in places such as Canada or Finland; in the latter country penetrations are limited to 20m of line and no incidents are known where divers have become lost while following recognised safety recommendations.

A diver in Finland preparing to venture beneath ice using a base-fed line

Base-fed penetrations are, of necessity, short for very good reasons. In the absence of communication by sight or sound, it is a real art to maintain the correct rope tension between two people. This is an essential factor which requires that the assistant develops a near intuitive understanding of the individual at the end of the line, judging when to let out line and when to retrieve. Confusion can easily arise if the tender misinterprets a signal or an accidental pull and pays out line instead of taking it in – a situation which can quickly become life-threatening. Of equal concern is that when the line is pulled, either by the diver or the assistant, there is a real risk of it being dragged into a crack or some other restricted area, through which the diver cannot pass on the return trip and from which it is impossible to recover the line. These places are often known as line traps for good reason. Appendix D contains further information on ice diving.

Other than below ice, it is better to lay line from a personal reel, recovering it on exit. The type of line varies with the application, but in general a nylon line is recommended, except for ice diving where a sturdy floating line made from a material such as polypropylene is useful. Nylon is strong, resists abrasion and sinks in water. Preferably, for ease of handling, the line should be of braided construction rather than woven or hawser-laid, which is particularly prone to kinking and unravels after being cut.

Depending upon its exact use, water temperature, visibility and the area of the world, the line is normally between 2mm and 6mm thick. Where water is warm and clear and current is not an influencing factor, thinner line is the norm. In temperate areas such as the British Isles, where the water temperature may be 7°C or less and visibility is frequently poor, thicker line is preferred – the diver must be able to feel it through thick neoprene gloves in these conditions.

In poor visibility thick line provides a massive psychological reassurance and it is also easier to attach directional line markings than on thin line. While the golden rule of line following is never to pull on the line, thicker line provides that option in an emergency and it will also resist the rigours of current, sharp rock and routine wear and tear for longer; it has been installed in a few caves around the world for these reasons. In a number of ebbing and flowing Bahamian blue holes heavy polypropylene line – despite its buoyant characteristics – is preferred because it can better withstand the marine growth which quickly engulfs and weighs the line down.

Where lines are to be left *in situ* for an extended period, and certainly where water is cold, the visibility is poor, or abrasion and flood damage are likely, thicker line is preferred. Other than beneath ice, nylon line – which sinks – is always the best choice

As a generalisation, though, floating line such as polypropylene should be avoided, certainly until the skills of line laying have been mastered. If too much nylon line is accidentally dispensed from a reel it generally settles harmlessly on the floor until reeled back in or the diver wraps it around a rock or whatever is conveniently to hand. Conversely, if too much floating line escapes it tends to create coils or loops which either form graceful arcs or, worse, spread like some malign spider's web, ready to ensnare the diver or his equipment.

Line should be laid from a specialised reel. This will vary in size and type according to the thickness of line it holds and, possibly, the markings or labels attached to the line. Terms such as primary, safety, gap or

To minimise the possibility of
entanglement, when laying line
it is ideally run off the reel
with one arm outstretched
and slightly to one side

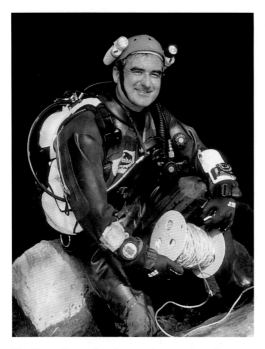

Handling polypropylene line requires practice – but training with this floating line can focus a diver's attention on the finer points of line laying

jump are often used to describe the function of a reel. Primary or penetration reels are most commonly used for laying a guideline from the cave entrance to the start of a permanent line, and are also used for original exploration. Gap or jump reels are used to lay line from a permanent main line to link with a separate fixed line in a complex system, perhaps in a side passage, while safety reels are carried for emergency use – in case of line loss or line breakage.

Reels must be of sound construction and are ideally operated with one hand. While swimming the line is deployed by the other hand, avoiding it catching on the centre spindle or becoming tangled on the carrying handle. Ideally, a reel should have a locking mechanism to prevent the line from being shed when not in use, and a simple method of attachment to the diver when being carried.

There are two main designs: closed frame and open frame. In a closed frame reel the entire drum is encased to avoid line spillage and line is deployed through a small opening. An open frame design is simpler but, if not handled with care, it can accidentally shed line, thereby contributing to entanglement. However, while an open frame may seemingly have a fundamental disadvantage it is generally

Small technical reels (right) are used to best advantage in warm water. In colder waters divers often wear gloves but, for better line control, they cut away the glove tips of the first fingers and thumb. Reels may be open or closed frame – closed frame reels may be more compact, but most overhead environment divers prefer to use open frame reels for their ease of handling.

Reels used by cave and mine divers in the UK are generally cheap, home-made varieties, normally without a locking mechanism (below). They are conspicuously larger than commercially available technical reels, mainly due to the thicker line that they are required to carry

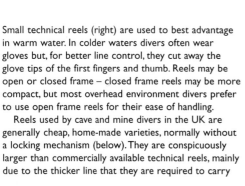

Line reels

Well-constructed reels have a bolt-snap connector for attachment to the harness, and a locking arrangement to prevent line from accidentally spilling into the water.

Examples here show a stainless steel technical reel with an adjustable brake/locking mechanism (above, left), a basic open frame reel with a locking wing nut and a plastic bead to hold the line taut against the metal line guide (centre), and an open frame reel showing the winding handle (above, right). Two reels have a snoopy loop attached to the end of the line.

The technical reel (right) lies beside a smaller spool, which is designed for absolute simplicity. Here, line is laid by running the spool from an outstretched finger

more versatile with respect to the size of line it will accommodate, with or without markers attached, and is easier to clear if the line jams or is tangled (very little, or nothing, can be done if this occurs inside a closed frame reel). No matter what type or size of reel is used it should never be excessively filled, owing to the risk of spillage or jamming when, for example, line is being recovered. As a rule of thumb, reels should not be over two-thirds full.

A final type of reel popular in warmer, more favourable cave environments is a finger spool. This small accessory allows the diver to cross a gap to another line or make a brief assessment of a side lead by running the spool from an outstretched finger.

It is highly desirable to place distance and direction markers on the line. In Europe lines are often 'tagged' using cable ties or insulation tape, generally at 5m or 10m intervals. Ideally, the tags are set in a clear numerical sequence with zero at dive base. In popular Florida caves prominent line markers are set at distances of 30m or more, while in extremely committing environments some divers also incorporate a directional colour and/or tactile coding sequence using knots or cable ties.

Using distance numbers complemented by orientation markers is invaluable to a stressed diver who is perhaps disorientated and urgently needs to establish the outward direction. By reading a number tag on a fixed or permanent line, then swimming to and checking the next, a diver can confirm direction and continue or turn back. Remember: the diver is already stressed and disorientated and may have low air reserves. If there is any element of doubt regarding the direction of travel, stress levels mount quickly. Incorporating an orientation code when tagging line provides an immediate indication of the outward direction, saving precious time for the diver in difficulty. Such a system may take time to arrange in our busy everyday lives, but there is no doubt that in a crisis such planning could be a lifesaver. Careful dive preparation is the key to safety.

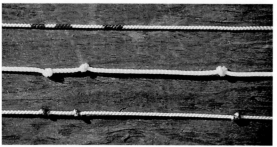

Permanently laid lines are found in most caves and mines, certainly beyond the cavern or easily accessible entrance section. Before using these lines it is prudent to consult local divers, as at many sites there is a deliberate policy to deter inexperienced divers by removing the line and the temptation to swim onwards. Experienced cave divers lay their own line until a link is made with the permanent one. As a rule these temporary lines should be removed again on exit, unless there is a good reason for leaving them in place. It is an unwritten rule that if a line is left *in situ* the diver takes responsibility for it until removal, and that any lines that are found are not interfered with.

While lines may remain sound for many years, for example in some mines, eventually they all degrade due to wear and tear or under the rigours of current or flooding. All permanent lines should be treated with suspicion and carefully examined along their entire length, at the very least by the first member

Marking lines

It is extremely advantageous to attach both distance and direction markings to lines over 3mm thick, particularly to those of hawser construction (markings are not easily seen or placed on thin technical line).

British cave divers generally use a combination of tie wraps/cable ties with separate short lengths of PVC electrical insulation tape to indicate the precise distance and direction from the dive base (top). However, attachments to the line may be unsuitable for use on a small technical reel with a restrictive line guide, as they may foul while being deployed or recovered.

Instead, indelible colour marks (which unfortunately will fade) may be used or, preferably, knots

of a team travelling along the route. If a line briefly disappears into a silt bank for a metre or so, it should be pulled free regardless of the resultant silting. Only by close examination can you be satisfied, or otherwise, that your outward journey will be uneventful. Frayed, broken and carelessly abandoned lines present a real danger to future explorers.

Line laying

Following and maintaining close contact with a line is essential; equally important is the way the line is laid to permit this. When installing a guideline, it should be kept reasonably taut (but not stressed) and a route should be chosen that will be easily negotiable on the way out, when conditions may have deteriorated. It is worth taking time over this, noting any peculiarities of the area, sediment banks, sharp rocks, undercuts or line traps into which the line may accidentally be pulled. In general, never deliberately lay the line along a ceiling: it is awkward to look up when your optimum view while swimming is down and, if you become caught in the line, above and behind is the most difficult position to extricate yourself from.

In popular Florida systems it may be common for several teams of divers to use the same cave at the same time. It is courteous for each team to keep its line away from others. Divers may share the same primary belay, perhaps on a log at the entrance, but thereafter each line should follow a different course with separate belays and placements as teams pass through the cavern zone. If it is necessary to cross the tunnel from one wall to the other, the second team should pass the line underneath the existing one – it is likely that the first team in will be the first team out, and the new installation should not compromise the exit.

Line laying is best regarded as a two-handed task. Ideally, the reel is held at a comfortable distance from the body to avoid entanglement with equipment, where it is operated with one hand while the other maintains the correct tension. It is important to carefully control the speed at which the line is dispensed, possibly using one finger to slow the spool's rotation. To ensure that the line remains in the best position for the outward journey it should be belayed at regular intervals. In this context

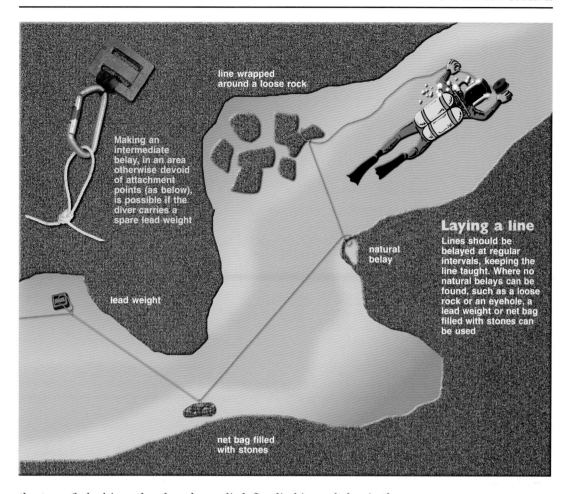

Making an intermediate belay, in an area otherwise devoid of attachment points (as below), is possible if the diver carries a spare lead weight

line wrapped around a loose rock

Laying a line
Lines should be belayed at regular intervals, keeping the line taught. Where no natural belays can be found, such as a loose rock or an eyehole, a lead weight or net bag filled with stones can be used

natural belay

lead weight

net bag filled with stones

the term 'belay' is rather loosely applied. In climbing a belay is thoroughly secure and can withstand body loading, while in the overhead environment belaying can mean any line attachment, from tying it onto a projecting flake of rock (possibly a semi-permanent installation) to a simple wrap around a pillar (a temporary installation).

The line can also be held in place by positioning it behind a boulder or placing a loose rock on top, as well as a number of other techniques. In the Americas this is referred to as making a placement. Where no suitable natural belays exist, the diver might tie the line to a block of lead or a net bag filled with cobbles or pebbles collected on the spot. If the section of tunnel has a floor of deep silt the diver might carry a silt screw, a short length of plastic piping fashioned to look like, and act in the same way as, a tent peg to securely hold the line in place, preferably above the silt. In a low tunnel it can be wedged between the floor and roof to prevent the line from drifting into a narrow undercut or line trap.

A technique routinely employed by European cave divers uses snoopy loops. These are similar to large elastic bands fashioned from rejected car inner tubes, which are cut neatly to form 1cm to 2cm wide loops. A prudent diver carries an easily accessible assortment of different diameters, in the UK normally

A belay created with a plastic canister, used as a buoy. For this technique the airbell must be large enough to retain the buoy in flood. The tag might be permanent or temporary

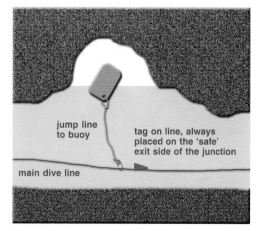

jump line to buoy

tag on line, always placed on the 'safe' exit side of the junction

main dive line

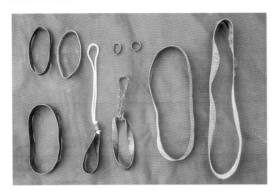

Snoopy loops

Snoopy loops are fashioned
from old pneumatic inner
tubes. Made in a variety of
sizes (above), they are used
for line belaying and are
invaluable for problem-solving.
The sequence below shows
how a snoopy loop is securely
attached to the main line. The
final image shows how a loose
rock can serve as an anchor

storing them around cylinders or the diver's thigh, where they are threaded under other snoopies on the bottle or leg.

To belay the line half the snoopy is passed around the line, then pulled back through the other part of the loop to leave it attached and hanging free to be stretched around a suitable rock or projection. The system can be extended by joining a similarly sized loop of nylon cord to the rubber snoopy, or adding a second snoopy to the first, to introduce a set distance between the dive line and the belay point. It is amazing what a snoopy loop will grip, even oval or rounded cobbles, and they have been effective at holding line in position for several years. They will, however, perish in due course and may be prone to detachment if the line is pulled: *never pull the line*.

The nature of the environment, visibility and the type of cord used will determine how often the line is, or should be, belayed. Where conditions are poor and the line is to be left in place it may be prudent to belay every few metres; in Europe about every 10m is advisable. In the UK preferred belay points are close to a wall or at floor level, though where conditions are favourable there is greater flexibility in placement.

Unless a diver is under supervision, complex caves and mines are places for fully certified and experienced cave divers only. If a wreck, cave or mine is being explored, surveyed or studied as part of an ongoing project, it is good practice to ensure that lines are clearly marked according to destination. The simplest method is to attach a dive slate with clear, legible writing. Ideally, different coloured line is used on different routes; all should be of consistent thickness to reduce potential confusion and improve overall safety.

However, thick line should be used on popular routes and thin line in offshoots. In Florida the main route in many caves is marked with heavy duty, 3mm thick 'goldline', which is a very distinctive colour. The guidelines in side passages are thinner and white and are always belayed several metres away from the main line. To enter these side tunnels the diver *must* deploy a gap or jump reel. This deliberate practice of separating side lines from lines in the main arterial route avoids potential confusion and, to a lesser extent, entanglement. If a diver wishes to conduct further work, or simply visit a side passage, it takes but a minute to lay line from a gap reel to reconnect with the side tunnel. Remember: *never jump a gap without leaving a continuous line in place*.

Technically, in the USA line and reel terminology is precise. A gap exists between the ends of two permanent lines, which are joined when a diver lays a temporary line during a dive. For example, one line may run from the surface to end in an airbell, while the ongoing line may be located a few metres further on; the gap must be bridged during

Running a jump reel in Mexico. In popular systems it is standard practice to install a permanently sited 'out' arrow on the end of a line, to indicate the direction of the nearest exit

the dive. A jump is the space between a continuing main line and the end of a permanent line in a side passage; when line is run from a jump reel this creates a T-junction on the main line.

Underwater line junctions can sometimes be extremely disconcerting, especially when exiting. Junctions must be kept simple to minimise stress and potential disorientation. In some caves, for example in the Bahamas, underwater T-junctions are common. Inexperienced divers should be extremely wary of such systems and clearly mark the outward (safe) side of every junction with a personal marker such as a plastic triangular-shaped 'arrow' or clothes peg. This is easily attached to the line, but *extreme* care must be taken to ensure that the arrow points in the correct, outward direction towards the exit. In Florida and Mexico, places where jumps are regularly made are prominently marked with a permanent 'double line arrow'. Here, two arrows are set close together in a row.

To avoid the proliferation of markers, potential confusion and (ultimately) unsightly litter, it is important that personalised arrows or pegs are removed on the outward journey. As well as confirming the dive order and letting the last person in the team know that all other members are safely accounted for, as they each placed a marker and personally removed it, it avoids confusion for divers in other teams. Clothes pegs can be used in complex caves to mark the furthest point of penetration on a

A small plastic arrow personalised with the owner's name or initials is securely attached to thin line (top). The lower marker is attached to thicker line, which may not permit additional wrapping. Care must be taken to ensure that arrows cannot accidentally fall from the line and that they always point 'out'

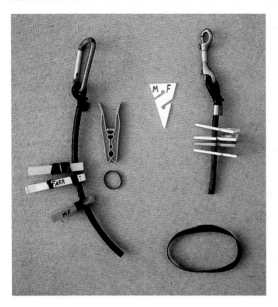

Line markers

A selection of traditional line markers (above). Small plastic arrows, correctly attached to avoid slippage, are preferable on thin line; clothes pegs are more suitable for thick line. Pegs (called clothes pins in the USA) may be carried on a short length of rubber tubing (top right).

To ensure that pegs do not accidentally fall apart they may be strengthened with small snoopy loops cut from bicycle inner tube. All pegs should be marked with the diver's initials.

If the supply of pegs has been exhausted, longer snoopy loops fixed directly onto the line can act as temporary 'out' markers

dive or to provide reassurance while setting up a traverse or loop dive. However, the diver must take care to ensure that markers cannot be displaced, perhaps by the water flow, and that they will not fall apart. Snoopy loops can also be used as reference points or for line marking at junctions.

Many mines and some caves, such as those of the Yucatán in Mexico, have multiple entrances, a complex layout and considerable potential for confusion. Line markers should always point to the exit; however, note that, after the midway point of a traverse between two entrances, arrows will no longer point back towards the divers' entrance, but now aim forwards to a different exit. The midpoint is frequently marked with a pair of arrows, set back to back to indicate opposite directions. It is essential that at least one member of the team (and preferably everyone) knows the layout of the second entrance – and that it is open and unobstructed, with a guideline which is connected to the permanent line deep inside. When attempting a traverse for the first time it is imperative that divers stick rigidly to the Rule of Thirds. The safe option of retracing the route in the event of confusion or a problem must be maintained. Be aware that an arrow may have been positioned incorrectly, or installed by a diver exploring the tunnel from the other direction; do not trust arrows implicitly.

Take careful note of the passage's physical characteristics on a regular basis. In a cave or mine this might include flow direction, passage size and shape, sediment type, prominent landmarks and permanently installed arrows. This action is commonly known as referencing which, with the use of a compass, is an extremely valuable aid to navigation. It is relatively straightforward to acquire the diving skills; it takes longer to develop an environmental awareness.

Safety reels

Although a diver should remain within arm's reach of the line, and in physical contact with it if visibility is poor, accidents can happen. If the line is lost it must be relocated as quickly as possible. If visibility has already deteriorated it could become worse still; the environment may be complex and the line could drift, especially if it is unbelayed or broken. Floating line, such as polypropylene, can easily rise from the floor, so know the characteristics of the line you are following and be aware of the way it was laid.

Presuming that you have not moved far from the point where you lost the line, finding it again ought to be straightforward. Cave divers carry a compact emergency safety reel for this eventuality. The size of this reel and how much line it holds depends on the environment; in the UK 10m of 3mm nylon is regarded as adequate for most situations but, clearly,

The end of the line may usefully include a loop, providing a simple, safe and very effective means of making a primary belay. This is achieved by running the line around a secure object and then passing the reel directly through the loop. Ensure, therefore, that the loop is large enough to comfortably accommodate the reel

Laying a thin line through the entrance section of the major cave El Moraig, on the Costa Blanca, Spain

more line is required in larger tunnels. The small safety reels adopted in Florida and Mexico contain a minimum of 30m and more usually 50m of line. It is essential to practise using a safety reel. In Britain it is strongly recommended that the safety line is fitted with a small lead drop weight and snoopy loop, ready for use. For further information on how to search for a lost line, see pages 88–92.

Never be tempted to use a safety reel for anything other than an emergency. Do not use it to jump gaps or to make short forays off the main line – prepare for these eventualities separately and use a gap reel or finger spool. If you have used your safety reel early in the dive it is no longer available in an emergency.

Any diver encountering a deployed gap reel or spool underwater should *never* remove or tamper with it: the line may be in use or placed ready for the following day. Do not use another diver's gap line unless they are fully aware of your dive plan; if you do leave the main line it is essential to fix personalised markers to be collected on exit.

Approaching a junction in Cenote Dos Pisos, Mexico. As road signs aid a motorist, placing 'out' arrows provides tremendous reassurance for a diver in a complex network with many junctions

Guidelines

Always:
- Lay a continuous line in any overhead environment
- Stay close to the line; if visibility is poor, maintain hand contact with it
- Use line appropriate to the environment and avoid floating line wherever possible
- Tag and colour code the line as appropriate
- Lay line with care, mindful of the return journey
- Mark junctions with personalised 'out' arrows or clothes pegs/pins (and remove them on exit)
- Carry an appropriate safety reel for the environment being explored
- Carry at least two knives or cutting tools (but cut line only as a last resort)

Never:
- Pull on a line, unless it is designated for that purpose
- Tamper with any permanently placed arrows
- Jump a gap without a line: the team must carry at least one jump or gap reel for every planned gap

Chapter five
Air Management

KNOWING when to terminate a dive, whether based on the air supply or any other factor, is crucial in an overhead environment. Air management requires the use of a suitable 'consumption rule', normally the Rule of Thirds.

In the Rule of Thirds the diver turns around after one-third of the air has been used. In theory, therefore, one-third is then used to regain the surface with one-third of the air still left in the cylinders at the end of the dive. No matter how experienced a diver is, or how many cylinders are carried, none of them should be breathed below a third on the inward journey. This creates an essential safety reserve to deal with any problem that might develop – provided that the diver is experienced and remains calm.

The Rule of Thirds creates the barest minimum reserve; in many situations a greater safety margin is preferable. Attention to detail, close monitoring of gauges and self-discipline are essential.

An analysis of incidents shows that a primary cause of fatality in flooded caves is a failure to maintain adequate air for a safe exit. For open water diving the size of the air reserve is based on the assumption that air-sharing with a buddy can be conducted to reach the surface. When explorers plan a dive into a cavern or deep into a cave, their reserves must be based on the possibility of sharing air with a buddy all the way out from the furthest penetration (possibly from the thirds turnaround point), and then (in the case of an exit at depth) up to the surface. This will entail using at least as much air from the donor's set as was consumed by both divers on the way in – and the act of sharing will induce additional problems such as stress or reduced visibility. As a direct consequence this will increase the breathing rate and cut into the safety margin of air. The Rule of Thirds must therefore *never* be exceeded.

Calculate the turnaround point for your gas supply before you commence your dive and write this clearly on your dive slate (you might also mark this on your pressure gauge). Starting a dive with 300 bar in your cylinders and using the Rule of Thirds, you would turn the dive on reaching 200 bar and end the dive with 100 bar in your cylinders.

If you start a dive with 230 bar, or some other number that is not readily divisible by three, begin the calculation by dropping to the nearest round number which *is* divisible by three and is therefore easier to work with. In this example, drop to 210 bar, which divides by three to give 70 bar. To complete the calculation correctly, *subtract the 70 bar from the original cylinder pressure*: 230 bar minus 70 bar equals 160 bar. You should therefore turn the dive on, or before, 160 bar and reach the surface with about 90 bar remaining in the cylinder – a good, healthy reserve!

It is extremely important that the calculation is made carefully as a simple mistake could mean that the dive is turned after using *more* than one-third of the starting air pressure. In the second example, carelessly subtracting 70 bar from the rounded down figure of 210 bar instead of the original cylinder pressure produces a turnaround figure of 140 bar. In reality, turning a dive at this point would mean that you have already breathed 90 bar to reach this point. The outward dive will require another 90 bar, leaving only 50 bar in the cylinders on exit. This is not an adequate emergency reserve and is considerably less than the accurately calculated 76.6 bar (based on the actual cylinder volume) which should be regarded as a minimum in this example.

Entering Wakulla Springs, Florida

Air management is critical, even in a favourable environment such as the Grotta Giusti spa, Tuscany, Italy. Gauges must be readily accessible, but must not dangle lower than necessary

The Rule of Thirds assumes that both divers in a team use the same sized cylinders filled to the same pressure, and that they breathe at the same rate. However, this is not always the case.

Divers often tell stories of people they know who 'don't seem to breathe' underwater, who manage to dive for longer on a given cylinder size than their colleagues can. Such a person, a fit young female diver for example, may adopt smaller capacity cylinders than her peers while retaining the same bottom time as the rest of the team. This is fine in open water, but transfer this scenario – where one person uses a smaller set of cylinders – into an overhead environment and the pair could be on course for disaster. Imagine the worse case where, at the point of thirds, the heavier breather needs to buddy-breathe out from the cave or cavern, sharing air from the smaller cylinder. They simply wouldn't make it.

Be aware that individuals have different consumption rates – and ensure that every member of a team carries an adequate reserve to assist an out-of-air companion.

Dissimilar cylinders or pressures

When divers have the same sized cylinders, establishing who has the most gas is straightforward: check the pressure gauges. When diving on differently sized cylinders, or when someone in the team has a poor fill, the situation is more complicated. The team must calculate its turnaround point, not necessarily based upon the smallest cylinder, but upon the individual with the smallest volume of gas. The team's penetration should therefore be limited to one-third of the smallest available volume. In Europe measurements are made in litres of free air: for example, a 10 litre cylinder pressurised to 200 bar contains 2,000 litres of free air, but if pressurised to 170 bar, it contains 1,700 litres of free air.

By applying the Rule of Thirds, the diver with the 200 bar cylinder would turn back having consumed some 666 litres of air (a turnaround at 134 bar). The diver with the smaller 170 bar cylinder would plan to turn after consuming 566 litres (at 114 bar). Simple logic suggests that whichever diver first reaches the turnaround point (the point of thirds) signals that an exit must be made. However, if the diver with the greater supply at the outset reaches the turnaround point first (the 666 litre diver, therefore having consumed 100 litres more air than the 566 litre diver) and then requires air-sharing, the buddy will probably not have sufficient reserves to bring them both back to safety. Divers must recognise this potential shortcoming at the planning stage.

The turnaround point must therefore always be controlled by the smaller air supply, not by the first to reach a third – in this example the dive must be turned after *either* diver has used 566 litres. If stress or other problems increases the breathing rate of the '200 bar cylinder diver', who

While exploring an intriguing site that may provide distractions it is essential to continuously monitor air supplies. The Gruta do Mimoso in the Bonito area of Brazil is one such place, as it contains a large cavern filled with cone-shaped stalagmites

Laying line
in Formoso
Springs, Brazil

Air management

- *Never* violate the Rule of Thirds
- The Rule of Thirds offers a bare minimum reserve in the overhead environment
- If cylinders of dissimilar sizes are used, *do not* give the largest to the heaviest breather

therefore uses air prodigiously, the dive should be called earlier (2,000 litres minus 566 equals 1,434 litres – in 'real' terms the pressure gauge would read 143 bar).

It is hopefully apparent that divers must be fully conversant with their cylinder size (its water capacity) and pressure so that they can consider and calculate these essential turnaround points. Additional information on calculating gas requirements appears in Appendix C.

As stated repeatedly – but it is so important that it will be repeated again – the Rule of Thirds creates the absolute barest minimum air reserve for diving in the overhead environment, and some situations require greater reserves.

Imagine, for example, that you going to dive into a tunnel in the same direction as the water flow – perhaps a siphon cave in Florida or Mexico or on the 'inflow' at a Bahamian blue hole. There is no way of knowing how strong the current may be inside the cave, and in the Bahamas you may not be aware of the precise stage of the tidal cycle, which controls the current. In this situation you would be well advised not to tackle the dive until you have gained a certain level of experience, and even then you should contemplate such dives with great conservatism.

Training agencies in the USA recommend that on a dive with so many unknowns the turn is made at one-sixth of the starting pressure. On a subsequent dive, using information gained from the first, a more conventional approach to reserves might be adopted – perhaps turning on one-quarter. Many cave divers in Florida now adopt scooters or DPVs (Diver Propulsion Vehicles) for their underwater activities, and have to carry sufficient gas to allow a swim out of the cave from the furthest point in the event of vehicle breakdown. Such dives are planned using the most conservative rules – perhaps that of Sixths.

Chapter six
Considering Depth

IN an overhead environment it matters little whether you are at 5m or 50m depth: you cannot make a direct emergency ascent. However, all problems are exacerbated by depth. Recreational dives are made to over 100m depth and record-breaking unassisted dives using open circuit apparatus exceed 270m. At these depths there is little margin for equipment failure or error.

From analysing fatalities in the overhead environment, particularly in cave diving, it is clear that depth is a primary factor. Training agencies worldwide, therefore, strongly recommend that inexperienced divers exercise self-discipline and restrict their activities to shallow water. For cavern diving, depths should not exceed 22m and certainly be no more than 30m. Even when qualified as a full cave diver a limit of 40m on air is appropriate. These figures were formulated for dives under optimum diving conditions in relatively warm water (20°C). Divers in colder water and with poor visibility should restrict activities to lesser depths.

Gas mixtures other than compressed air offer considerable benefits. Nitrox – a variable composition breathing mixture with reduced nitrogen and increased oxygen – is widely accepted in the leisure, technical and cave diving world, and other gas mixtures will eventually have a similar role at greater depths. However, it is abundantly clear that using these gases safely and responsibly requires considerably more knowledge than when diving on air. As this book serves only as an introduction to the overhead environment, gas mixtures are beyond its scope and discussions are restricted to using air.

Gas consumption

The deeper you dive, the more gas you consume with every breath. At 10m depth the pressure is 2 bar, twice that at the surface, and gas is used at twice the surface rate. At 40m the pressure is 5 bar and air is consumed five times faster. Because the supply is breathed at a faster rate, it follows that a lot more gas has to be carried and that divers must be more efficient in their conduct to avoid wastage. However, breathing must continue slowly and regularly.

At depth a number of considerations, mainly relating to complex issues associated with partial pressures, must be addressed. These, in turn, raise

Two divers begin their descent of the Chasm in Piccaninnie Ponds, Australia. There is a mandatory depth restriction of 36m at this most attractive, clear water site, which has claimed the lives of two divers over the years

Heading deeper into Gruta do Mimoso, in the remote Mato Grosso of Brazil. When the nearest decompression chamber is 14 hours distant, it is even more important to be careful

health-related and other physiological concerns.

Partial pressures cannot be ignored; divers are constantly exposed to their effects and must have an awareness of them at a basic level. Air at sea level exerts a pressure of 1 bar and for our purposes comprises 0.79 bar nitrogen (N_2) and 0.21 bar oxygen (O_2). Because each gas is a part of the whole, its component pressure is termed a partial pressure and is represented by the symbol PP; when related to a specific gas such as oxygen this is represented by the symbol PPO_2, while nitrogen would be PPN_2.

Each 10m of depth increases the total pressure on the diver by 1 bar, so at 10m the pressure on the diver has doubled and the partial pressure for O_2 also doubles, to 0.42 bar. At 20m the partial pressure rises to 0.63 bar, at 30m 0.84 bar and so on. The same relationship applies to all gases; in this example the nitrogen content at 10m depth becomes 1.58 bar and at 20m 2.37 bar. It is crucial that the effects of partial pressure at depth for each gas are understood.

Oxygen

Oxygen is essential to support life, but when it is breathed at high pressures it becomes increasingly narcotic, as does nitrogen and other gases. Excessive exposure to oxygen is dangerous and breathing pure oxygen at depths in excess of 10m (2 bar) rapidly causes oxygen poisoning (also known as oxygen toxicity). The warning signals of impending toxicity include visual and hearing disorders such as tinnitus (ringing in the ears), nausea, twitching, irritability, dizziness or even convulsions. When breathing air, the same critical partial pressure threshold is reached at a depth of 90m (10 bar).

Divers must be extremely cautious with oxygen and for technical deep diving it is recommended that its partial pressure does not exceed

1.4 bar. Pure oxygen should only be used at depths of 6m or less, and then only for limited periods; at 6m pure oxygen has a PPO_2 of 1.6 bar – the maximum acceptable toxic limit. Of course, gas mixtures dilute the effects of oxygen and this is why divers on air can safely descend to 66m – the depth at which the 21 per cent of oxygen found in air reaches a PPO_2 of 1.6 bar.

The following information indicates the safe dive times in minutes at different partial pressures of oxygen. There is a distinction between single and multiple dives: a single dive with a PPO_2 of 1.2 bar is safe for up to 210 minutes, but a second dive on the same day would be limited to only 30 minutes. Multiple dives have cumulative effects and it is unsafe to repeat long dives which, singly, are within the safe oxygen limits, but together will exceed the daily maximum.

Oxygen limits on dive times

PPO_2 (bar)	Single dive (min)	Daily max. (min)
1.6	45	150
1.5	120	180
1.4	150	180
1.3	180	210
1.2	210	240
1.1	240	270
1.0	300	300

During prolonged oxygen decompression stops it is highly advisable to take a five-minute 'air break' (a switch to breathing normal compressed air) at 25 minute intervals. Indeed, if there is any doubt about the onset of oxygen toxicity the diver should take an air break.

Transporting decompression gas also requires careful planning. Several fatalities have occurred when divers have accidentally changed to an oxygen-rich supply at too great a depth. For wreck diving it may be best to carry all the decompression gas throughout the dive, and on some committing cave diving explorations where decompression is involved – perhaps on the far side of a long or deep sump as the diver ascends to the air surface – carrying the decompression cylinder to depth en route is unavoidable.

Preparing to dive in
Coves del Pirata, Mallorca

However, in the majority of caves and mines decompression cylinders can be attached to the dive line at the required depth during the inward journey, in much the same way as stage cylinders are on long dives (see p33). Cylinders containing a high percentage of oxygen and the regulators intended for use on these must be conspicuously labelled. To prevent accidental use, fitting a mouthpiece guard to the regulator is prudent. Both cylinders and regulators must be 'oxygen clean' – even slight contamination from dirt, lint or hydrocarbons runs the risk of an explosion.

Carbon dioxide

Divers should never be tempted to hold their breath, skip-breathe or restrict their normal respiration cycle in any way as this builds up carbon dioxide levels in the blood. Carbon dioxide (CO_2) in the blood is essential to trigger normal breathing, but an accumulation can be dangerous and with little or no warning, in extreme cases, it may cause a CO_2 blackout. The gas occurs naturally in air at about 0.03 per cent; the partial pressure produced by concentrations of only 0.05 per cent is toxic and greater than 0.1 per cent is lethal.

Carbon dioxide may accumulate in a number of ways. Any breathing system that has an area of dead space where gas that is breathed out does not leave the confines of the equipment, such as the volume between the mouth and exhaust valve, can permit re-inhalation. Full face masks may appear to be the prime culprits, but restrictive clothing or a harness (causing shallow breathing), or an inefficient regulator, may pose a hazard.

The most inconspicuous accumulation is actually within the respiratory system. If you pant through breathlessness, breathe shallowly in an attempt to conserve gas or do not fully exhale, CO_2 builds up in the dead spaces found in the airways leading to the lungs – shallow breathing only pushes the gas into the windpipe and the next breath inhales in again. Breathe properly with deep, regular breaths at all times.

A rise in CO_2 levels may be signalled by a headache and/or breathlessness. These symptoms may subsequently increase and lead to confusion and, in extreme cases, a loss of consciousness. However, other factors may mask these effects. For example, physical stress caused by swimming in fast currents or the sheer length of a swim combined with mental stress may produce the same symptoms. A CO_2 build-up may not appear to be the most important consideration at the time, but nevertheless it is important to counteract it.

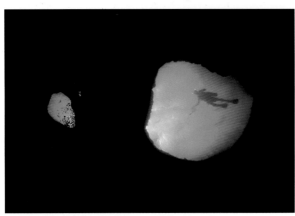

If you feel that CO_2 is affecting you, as a matter of urgency stop physical exertions and try to relax. Concentrate upon staying calm and regaining a controlled breathing pattern; deep, controlled breaths will flush excess CO_2 from your system. If an inefficient regulator caused the problem, take long, slow, deep breaths and avoid sharply sucking at the air supply. Control your stress level.

It is far better to avoid a CO_2 problem by ensuring that you and your equipment are in the best condition possible. Carry plenty of air and stick to the Rule of Thirds and your original dive plan.

Entering a blue hole in Mastic Sound on the Bahamian island of Andros. Where the water is clear and warm, divers may be tempted to venture ever deeper and narcosis becomes more of a threat

Nitrogen

All gases are toxic at depth, but nitrogen is a major concern – it is imperative that its effects are minimised.

Increasing depth increases the partial pressure of nitrogen, and this can produce a narcotic effect. The onset of nitrogen narcosis is insidious; it can affect both mind and body, and no one is immune. Symptoms are well documented: personality and mood change, a general euphoria and apparent 'drunkenness', plus some divers experience fear and anxiety. Physical symptoms include dizziness, loss of coordination, numbness in the lips, and changes in sight such as tunnel vision. In severe cases this may lead to loss of consciousness. As narcosis arises with little or no warning, catching the diver unawares, it is extremely important to be constantly alert for the symptoms.

Ascending to a shallower depth (where the nitrogen partial pressure is lower) will solve the problem, but this option may not be available in an overhead environment. Some divers experience narcosis at only 30m depth; at greater depth acclimatisation is important and this must be undertaken gradually. Experience does not increase tolerance or remove the symptoms of narcosis, but with practice it seems that individuals can greatly improve their 'coping skills'. Like anything else, acclimatisation can be broken by a lay-off from diving: always know your limits and stay within them.

The factors most likely to induce nitrogen narcosis are:

- Alcohol
- Drugs
- Heavy workload
- Fatigue
- Stress and anxiety
- Rapid descent
- Low temperature
- Poor health and physical condition

Decompression and decompression sickness

For anything other than the shallowest of dives to less than 10m, all ascents require decompression. Ascending divers should make a safety stop at 3m or 6m to give time for the body to shed excess gas absorbed in the blood at depth. For

Cylinders must be conspicuously marked, leaving no doubt about their contents

Returning from a deep exploratory dive in Formoso Springs, Bonito, Brazilian cave diver Gilberto Menezes is carrying two front-mounted stage cylinders

long or deep dives it is essential that divers are fully aware of the physiological implications of pressure and prepare accordingly.

When we breathe, gases dissolve into our bloodstream and body tissues. Under compression at depth a greater amount of gas is dissolved; when the pressure decreases during ascent these are released again. While oxygen and carbon dioxide are quickly absorbed and released, nitrogen takes longer to dissolve and be discharged. If pressure is reduced too quickly during an ascent the dissolved nitrogen is decompressed and released too quickly, inducing decompression sickness (commonly known as the bends).

Nitrogen absorption and elimination is affected by three factors:

A dive profile

This computer-generated graph of a cave dive in the Émergence du Ressel, France, was made by the Dutch cave diver José de Veer and shows how useful computers are for dive planning.

Starting from the water surface (the top left-hand corner), José swam at a relaxed speed covering 100m every 6 or 7 minutes. After about 18 minutes the passage descended to –45m and the diver turned for the exit at 25 minutes. Just after this point (at the yellow triangle) the computer indicated a minimum safe ascent time of 5 minutes, including any necessary decompression stops. However, because the return required swimming for a period at a shallower depth (about 8m) the requirement for decompression was actually eliminated at 43 minutes. Even so, José made an additional safety stop at 56 minutes, just before the final ascent.

When planning dives the swimming speed can be used to calculate how far the diver can travel into a cave in a given time, and the cave survey will indicate the depths involved while following the passage. These values, and others, can be used by dive computers to help plan and execute a safe dive

Pressure gradient
The greater the pressure difference between lungs, blood and body tissue, the greater the uptake or elimination of nitrogen.

Tissue type
Blood, fat, muscle and bone absorb nitrogen at differing rates. Muscle has one of the fastest rates of gas absorption and release due to its extensive capillary beds. Fat, with fewer capillaries, accumulates and sheds gas slowly.

Blood flow
The rate of blood flow varies between different organs and parts of the body and, as a consequence, the rate of absorption and elimination varies from these areas. Strenuous exercise or exertion, either before, during or following a dive, increases the rate of blood flow to tissues and may induce or increase decompression sickness.

To avoid decompression sickness divers must control their ascent, allowing time for nitrogen to escape from the blood and tissues. After a long or deep dive this may involve staying at a specific depth for a certain time calculated using dive tables or a computer – a decompression stop.

Most divers use a computer to calculate what decompression is required. Software packages and sophisticated underwater instrumentation have removed much of the stress that previously accompanied long or deep dives. With their multitude of read-outs it is very tempting to place complete trust in these units, but they must not be regarded as a panacea for decompression information. They are tools and, like any other equipment, are no better or worse than the person using them.

If computers are operated according to manufacturers' instructions and within their design parameters, their benefits are immense. The decompression model or algorithm in the computer is a mathematical and logical formula with variables of depth and time. Traditional dive tables base decompression advice on the assumption that the entire dive was spent at maximum depth – the 'square profile'. However, divers normally spend only a small fraction of their time at the deepest point achieved, which means that during most of the dive the diver absorbs less nitrogen than tables assume. Computers update every few seconds and present a profile of the *actual* dive and the decompression required to compensate for it, including the time spent at shallow depths. Computers are vastly more flexible than tables and frequently permit more accurate planning.

Conversely, computers have some disadvantages: divers must correctly read and understand the information displayed, then act upon it. Some divers become so reliant upon computers that they neglect to carry tables for emergency use. Furthermore, traditional tables round up depths or times and, because they use a 'maximum depth for the entire dive' rule, as mentioned above, they also err on the safe side when a diver spends any time in the shallows during an otherwise deeper dive.

All that computers (or tables) contain is information about the relationship between depth and time. Though this is sophisticated, there is

no account taken of a diver's age, exertion, gender, hydration levels or the water temperature. Divers must add their own safety factors based on the specific environment they are in, their physiological state and previous dive profiles – just as they were taught when introduced to tables.

A solo diver should carry a second computer to check the accuracy of the first. In the event of a discrepancy, always err on the side of safety

For individuals embarking beyond the limits of 'no-decompression' diving the overriding concern is returning without having suffered decompression sickness, rather than exiting the water in the fastest time. Follow computer instructions carefully; do not compromise on safety. Multiple ascents and descents in a cave must be treated with caution; buoyancy and rate of ascent must be carefully regulated.

To avoid problems ascend slowly at never more than 10m per minute and, no matter where you are diving, make a safety stop for a minute or two at 3m or 6m, regardless of any decompression obligation. Likewise, spending a little longer than computers advise at your shallowest decompression stop is wise and, if practical, also consider additional stops at depth.

When diving at altitude, perhaps at 300m above sea level or higher, be extra vigilant and cautious. Computers are invaluable, but an altitude adjustment may be required. Failure to address this issue can result in erroneous data being displayed, which will greatly increase the risk of decompression sickness.

Hydrating is important before any long or deep dive, not only in warm climes. Drink lots of water!

Divers must take full responsibility for their own actions and safety. Even if your buddy carries a similar dive computer, consider redundancy – in a confined environment accidental damage is not uncommon. In remote situations carry either a second computer or, preferably, a watch, depth gauge and tables.

Decompression sickness may be classified into two types:

Type 1 causes 'pain only', with pain manifesting itself at or near a joint and possibly accompanied by fatigue, a lack of mental awareness or irritable behaviour. In turn the diver may suffer a 'skin bend' – a mild rash or itching.

Type 2 is more severe and is associated with damage to or severe effects upon the central nervous system. Symptoms may involve pain or paralysis, a headache, shortness of breath, dizziness or unconsciousness. Severe cases of decompression sickness may also be accompanied by a gas embolism (a bubble of gas obstructing a blood vessel).

Recognising the onset of decompression sickness is essential. Symptoms occur with the following frequencies:

1. Local joint pain	89% of divers
of these: leg	30%
arm	70%
2. Dizziness (the staggers)	5.3%
3. Paralysis	2.3%
4. Shortness of breath	1.6%
5. Extreme fatigue	1.3%
6. Unconsciousness	0.5%

The time between the end of the dive and the onset of symptoms also varies:

within 30 minutes	50% of divers experience symptoms
one hour	85%
three hours	95%
six hours	99%

A suspected bend

After any deep operation divers must be alert for decompression sickness in themselves and their companions. It has frequently been observed that individuals deny to themselves that they may have a problem, but a good buddy will act immediately if uncharacteristic behaviour is observed.

Immediate action is required if decompression sickness is suspected, as symptoms may be progressive. While medical advice is sought, undertake therapeutic treatment: keep calm, reassure the patient and implement basic first aid. A key action is to administer oxygen as quickly as possible; if a pure source is unavailable, decompression gas or nitrox is an excellent fall-back. Rest the diver in a horizontal position and, if the patient is capable of taking fluid, provide a drink of water (preferably containing glucose). In remote areas and on deep dives where professional aid is unavailable, team members should plan for all eventualities and consider whether in-water treatment might be conducted.

Forewarned is forearmed and, as well as knowing the remedial actions to take, have contact names and telephone numbers for emergency medical assistance readily accessible.

Contributing factors

It is obviously better to avoid decompression sickness than to suffer its consequences and some individuals are more prone than others due to their health or general activities. Factors increasing the likelihood of developing decompression sickness include:

- Depth (in the USA approximately 70% of divers treated have been below 25m)
- Time spent at depth
- Rapid ascent rate
- Poor physical fitness
- High body fat
- Exercise undertaken before, during or after the dive
- Repetitive dives (a high percentage of divers treated develop symptoms after repetitive dives)
- Multiple ascents (beware of irregular dive profiles, especially in cave diving)
- Dehydration
- Taking alcohol or drugs (including commonly used decongestants such as Sudafed®)
- Previous injury
- Smoking
- Vasoconstriction

A diver's health and lifestyle are therefore extremely important. Drugs to avoid may include prescribed medication, because at depth the increased pressure may alter its effect in an unpredictable manner. Refrain from drinking alcohol the night before diving, and certainly not to excess; it remains in the body for many hours and, apart from causing a hangover, alcohol contributes directly to dehydration and anxiety. Substances such as caffeine and nicotine should also be minimised as these lead to dehydration.

Significant dehydration can occur during a normal dive. Water is lost due to breathing dry air and immersion also causes water loss. If a diver is already dehydrated before the start of a dive these further water losses can cause a substantial reduction in blood volume, which in turn decreases the rate at which nitrogen is removed from tissues. Further, as blood thickens it becomes stickier and more likely to clot around bubbles, and this slows and impedes their movement to the lungs – which is where they can be filtered and removed. Eating fatty foods within a few hours of a dive can increase blood fat, which has the same effect.

Many experts recommend drinking glucose-enriched liquids immediately before, after and

Decompressing using a stage cylinder. How these are carried and sited requires careful planning

even during the course of a long duration dive. Fresh water is recommended, perhaps weakly diluted with apple juice (this is recognised as a neutral, beneficial drink in the UK, while Gatorade® is popular in the USA), but avoid citrus drinks and isotonic liquids which contain sodium. Hydrating (drinking lots of water) well before a dive can greatly improve how you feel afterwards.

Do not underestimate the effect of cold upon decompression. When we become cold, blood is diverted away from the skin surface and extremities to prevent heat loss. As a result, some blood vessels constrict and this delays normal respiratory exchange with, and the elimination of accumulated gases from, cells.

Hard exercise underwater and the accompanying possibility of raised carbon dioxide levels – together with fatigue – increases the risk of nitrogen narcosis and decompression sickness. Similarly, avoid strenuous exertion at the end of the dive, when you may have to climb into a boat or up a steep bank. Unless the water is excruciatingly cold, spend five minutes or more at the surface before struggling back to civilisation with a load of heavy equipment. Rest as much as possible immediately following a dive, but avoid alcohol.

Smoking and the effects of nicotine have many adverse effects. Smoking directly affects the oxygen-carrying capability of red blood cells, reducing oxygen content and increasing carbon dioxide and carbon monoxide.

Diving is a wonderful, physically beneficial recreation, but with advancing years a touch of conservatism is advisable, certainly where deep diving is concerned. However, it is clear that fitness is the most important aspect and divers of all ages should take care of their cardiovascular system. All the foregoing factors are compounded by stress, poor health and a poor physical condition; stay fit and healthy to give yourself all the advantages that you can. It is a sobering thought, but worth reflection, that in the USA statistics suggest that the fattest twenty-five per cent of the diving population, as measured by skin-fold thickness, have a tenfold increase in the incidence of decompression sickness. Anything that impinges on health decreases the safety margin assumed by dive tables and computers.

Plan deep dives carefully, use the best equipment, hydrate properly before the dive, keep warm, and minimise effort.

Laying line in
Gran Cenote, Mexico

Gas embolism

A gas embolism – the production of gas bubbles in blood vessels or tissues – occurs as a result of a too rapid depressurisation on ascent. The symptoms are generally traumatic and take different forms depending upon where the injury occurs and where the gas then moves to.

Basic training teaches us that a rapid ascent or holding breath can result in acute damage to the lungs, because the air expands while it is trapped. Much the same is true of gas bubbles forming in a blood vessel. If the bubble is large enough to block an artery feeding a vital organ, this is quickly starved of its blood supply; if it is in the brain the diver may lose coordination or become dizzy, and paralysis may rapidly lead to unconsciousness and possibly death.

Emphysema is another form of gas embolism, whereby air escapes into body tissues. This has several manifestations, often involving acute breathing difficulties, but may become apparent as subcutaneous emphysema with localised swelling in the neck. All instances of gas embolism must be dealt with extremely urgently; the only treatment is recompression therapy in a chamber. As with other pressure-related incidents, the casualty will benefit from breathing oxygen.

Renowned cave divers Rob Palmer and Rob Parker decompressing after an exploration dive in a Bahamian blue hole in 1981. Equipment and techniques have changed considerably since that time and today all divers would use wings, and dive computers are universal. No matter how well equipped the diver, no one can afford to be complacent about depth and a safety stop should always be made

On longer, deeper dives, such as in Wakulla Springs, Florida (left), divers sometimes install an underwater habitat in which they can conduct part of their decompression. The vessel at Wakulla could be winched in stages towards the surface during decompression, meaning that divers did not need to leave it to attain their next stop. On major expeditions to deep caves tremendous logistical and team support is required.

The habitat used at the Émergence du Ressel, France, in 1999 (below) was more basic, allowing divers to stand in a man-made airbell formed within an upturned refuse bin

Decompression etiquette

Divers exiting from a cave have priority over those entering. It follows that those undertaking decompression have the right of way over those making a descent. At busy sites it is a sad fact of life that some consideration must be given to the security of unattended equipment, even that installed for decompression.

This chapter has presented only a basic overview of a complicated – though fascinating – subject. More detailed information can be found in diving medical texts (see Appendix A).

Chapter seven
Stress

IN an ideal world divers would read all the diving literature available, seek professional advice, buy the most appropriate equipment and gain experience as they progress under the tutelage of revered mentors. However, we all make mistakes. If we are sensible, we learn from these; with maturity comes the realisation that learning is an ongoing process and we need to foster an open mind and cultivate a healthy attitude. Psychology is a complex area of study, but it plays a crucial role in diving. We need to understand ourselves – *and understanding and controlling stress is as important as any other training.*

Stress is a complex subject, but if we are determined to learn from the mistakes of others, it is one that we must consider carefully. Underwater, we are in an alien environment and life is only supported by our specialised breathing equipment. The further and deeper we progress into this realm, the more committed we become and the greater the potential for stress. Some people appear to cope better than others, but no one is immune. No two people react in the same way and what might be a stressful situation for one may be perfectly normal for another. Our tolerance for stress varies according to age, experience, health and fitness, equipment, the situation and the nature of a buddy – and these are only a few of the factors involved. Stress figures prominently in incident analyses and, next to diver error, stress is the number one killer in diving.

A little stress is good as it ensures that you pay attention to detail and do not become complacent, but – clearly – too much stress is bad. Anything above a minimal level of stress quickly destroys any enjoyment and satisfaction in the dive. Some unsettling, momentary event may trigger a heightened sense of anxiety. This nervousness results in an increased breathing rate, and in turn this may trigger a chain reaction which, if not controlled, can quickly lead to panic. Once this threshold is reached there is little doubt that the diver's life is in serious jeopardy.

Panic is without question the ultimate state of mental narrowing. There is no longer a relationship between what is happening to the diver and what the person is doing about it. Panic may lead to an emergency ascent and an embolism; panic breathing can abnormally expand the lungs, which in turn press upon and restrict blood flow to the heart. In the worse cases this may interrupt the flow of oxygenated blood to the brain and lead to unconsciousness – and the diver may drown.

As stress increases, the ability to analyse and respond in an appropriate manner diminishes. With increased stress yet more mistakes are made and this becomes a rapidly escalating vicious circle that must be broken with the utmost urgency. Recognising stress at an early stage is therefore important; the more advanced the condition, the harder it is to deal with – and the panic that follows is even harder or impossible to control.

Tackling stress

Stress is a condition linked to specific events within the diver's environment, resulting in specific behaviour in the diver. A tolerance for stress is developed by learning and practising appropriate techniques to counter these situations.

Psychologists know that it is not what you do to people that makes them stressed, but what you do compared with what they *expect* to happen. People exhibit greater tolerance to stress if it is of a type and intensity that they expect to encounter; if they encounter something

Any action that can be taken to increase safety margins will decrease stress in the event of an incident. One example is attaching a small slate to the line on the out (safe) side of any junction, thereby increasing the speed at which the outward direction can be positively identified.

These slates have been made using small sections of plastic. They are cheap, easy to make or obtain, and can be attached using a snoopy loop or cable tie

Just one careless movement may cause the loss of visibility. The importance of laying a line, even during the shortest excursion into the overhead environment, is readily apparent

Anticipation, training, practice: the keys to coping with stress

unexpected they are far more prone to succumb. It is therefore extremely important for a diver to anticipate possible sources of stress.

There are two main forms of stress: psychological and physiological, affecting mind and body respectively. There is little doubt that these interact closely and either may trigger a reaction in the other. Psychological stress is not always caused by the environment; completely unrelated factors may be at work, such as family worries or self-doubt generated by commitments made to some third party. The ego may be affected if a diver perceives that he or she is the weak link in the team. Clearly, environmental components – darkness, depth, time – all contribute to stress.

Physical stress is perhaps easier to understand. The water may be very cold and the dive long enough that you feel its effects; you may have been tired and physically weary even before the dive started. Perhaps the dive is deep and visibility, poor to start with, has deteriorated further. Becoming disorientated, losing the line (a major cause of stress) or buoyancy, experiencing an equipment malfunction or entanglement; any factor can tip the balance and induce stress.

With a little forethought we can do something about physical stress, perhaps by waiting for the water to warm up or increasing our protection against cold. We can ensure that we are in peak condition rather than starting out tired, and reduce the workload by enlisting extra help. Problems with depth can be overcome by undertaking build-up dives, carrying more air or perhaps using a different gas mix. Worries about weighting can be reduced with reliable, redundant buoyancy, and there are several approaches to minimising problems with silt.

A mature, well-trained diver holds a balanced view of physical and psychological stress and the ability to cope with these. Nevertheless, the potential for stress is always present – but the good diver anticipates this and is ready to rectify problems or retreat at the first sign. By contrast, an inexperienced, poorly trained diver is ill-prepared for trouble and has much less capacity to cope before matters escalate beyond the point of control.

Stress can result in a diver making basic mistakes; emergency skills and techniques are even more vulnerable, but these are what are required in this situation. Unlike basic skills, emergency procedures are not routinely practised – a factor addressed by what the military calls 'over-learning'. Apart from developing the ability to anticipate problems and undertaking additional training, we must practise, practise and practise until we can accomplish the task without thinking. There is a tremendous difference between achieving a skill once only and being able to do it correctly every single time. Over-learning takes the doubt out of performance under stress – but remember that once mastery has been achieved, it still has to be maintained.

The keys to coping with stress are therefore anticipation, training and practice.

Thinking under pressure

It is essential that you think clearly in a stressful situation where the innate human reaction is to do something urgently – fight or flight. Neither option serves well in the overhead environment. If a stressful situation suddenly develops the most important first step is to allow your brain to engage. Do not rush headlong at the task: *stop, compose yourself, take two or three calming breaths, and think before continuing.*

In stressful conditions ask yourself: 'What is wrong? What is the best thing to do?' This may only require a second or two; it may take longer, but observation and analysis are crucial. Time spent thinking will be the most important of your life. In a threatening situation, rather than beginning to panic, *think* – for example, in an out-of-air emergency quickly check to see if your cylinder valve has been accidentally closed, while thinking ahead to the next step and signalling your buddy.

If everything else on the dive has gone to plan, you have plenty of air and light available. So, calm down and regain a near normal breathing rate. Visibility is deteriorating, so orientate yourself. Most entanglements can be cleared in a minute or less, but in the worse case you may need to cut yourself free. This is a critical step, so it is essential that you have made a thorough assessment of the situation and are in complete control before you make the cut.

Incidents become critical when you lose control and secondary, perhaps worse problems arise. Training and practice generate confidence and increase the probability that

In poor visibility, dives are effectively solo. Such conditions are routinely encountered in the British Isles and divers become used to them, but they can be extremely stressful for individuals who normally dive in clear water as part of a team. If the line is loose or badly laid in a small passage there is the added possibility of a line trap developing. Constricted conditions are always committing

Losing visibility when using a scooter can be critical. Downblast from a propeller immediately disturbs the silt and compromises the use of the machine

you can take appropriate action. Lack of awareness and training quickly results in a catalogue of errors. The diver slides into an 'incident pit' where mishaps are cumulative and there is rarely an escape.

Safe, enjoyable diving requires that you do not make a mistake in the first place. Taking an analogy from pilot training: the superior pilot is one who uses superior judgement to avoid situations that would require his superior skill in an emergency.

No matter how good you are, avoid problems. Also, remember that your capabilities may vary from day to day, as will those of your companions. If you are diving as a team, keep an eye on each other, even before entering the water. Just as you must be environmentally aware, be fully tuned with your partners; if stress becomes apparent, adjust the dive accordingly. The best dive teams are composed of individuals who know and understand each other well. They share similar experiences and trust each other completely – and as a result suffer less stress.

Reducing stress

- Cultivate a healthy attitude
- Train thoroughly and practise techniques regularly
- Anticipate likely problems and practise solving them
- Gather as much information as you can about the proposed dive
- Choose companions with similar experience who all trust each other
- Ensure that all equipment is sound and appropriate for the dive
- Follow all general rules and procedures
- Dive within your limits
- If a problem occurs, *stop, breathe and think before doing anything*

Chapter eight
Dive Planning

DIVE planning is fundamental in the overhead environment. Divers, individually and as a team, must be more precise with procedures than in open water. This requires a particular mindset, central to which is attention to detail.

Most, if not all things that might go wrong on a dive can be anticipated. Careful planning – including information gathering, logistics, reviewing scenarios, discussion and decision-making – serves to prevent the majority of problems from developing. A team with an effective plan is more capable of dealing with unexpected events and can rectify small problems before they become critical.

During preparations an experienced overhead diver will know where to find the necessary information – or if not, will know a person who can. On a training course an instructor makes these assessments based upon considerable personal experience and having seen how other students react. Further, the instructor will be on hand to closely monitor and ensure that the student can complete the dive safely. However, once a student moves beyond that stage of instruction, he or she must deal with all the complexities of dive planning without this support. Some data may

be inappropriate, and so-called experts may offer advice and opinion which must be thoroughly evaluated before taken up or rejected. This is perhaps the danger period, when the depth and effectiveness of training become apparent. Inexperienced divers should progress cautiously, preferably consulting their instructor, and reflect carefully upon each dive.

Redundancy and self-reliance should underpin all preparations, even for team dives, though divers at this stage should not carry too much equipment – there is a fine balance between carrying too much and carrying the minimum for a comfortable yet safe dive. The concept

A group meeting prior to a recreational dive at Grotta Giusti, Italy. Dive briefings are crucial in any environment

of simplicity or KISS (Keep It Simple, Stupid) is important, both with respect to equipment and the dive plan. The latter should be kept simple, clear and concise, allowing problems to be readily identified and rectified.

Planning depends upon the environment. In many British sumps, given their poor environmental conditions – confined, murky, cold water – it is impractical to dive with a buddy. Although two, three or more cave divers may regroup beyond a sump, it is likely that they dived solo, perhaps several minutes apart. If they are in the water at the same time, all divers must be fully aware of the dive plan and what to do if anyone else requires assistance; in particular, they should understand any limitations with their companion's kit configuration. Even so, a buddy in these conditions is something of a bonus rather than the norm.

In more favourable situations – spacious, clear, warm water – a two- or three-man dive team is more usual. In this environment it is essential to discuss at length the general and precise aims of the dive, the team limits and individual roles. Team diving is most effective when everyone possesses similar experience and a rapport based upon years of interaction, perhaps with an extensive array of communication skills and well matched in the equipment and techniques being used. Solo diving, while often frowned upon under good diving conditions, is nevertheless possible. In this case the diver should consider carrying a separate 'buddy-bottle' – a spare set of equipment for emergency use.

Whatever diving is undertaken the individual should evaluate his or her ability to undertake the dive, and that of any buddy. Ego and peer pressure must not be underestimated. If a diver is part of a team that has invested considerable time and effort setting up a project, he or she may experience considerable pressure to undertake the dive despite some personal reticence. Divers in the USA attempt to minimise these pressures during both planning and the dive using the rule:

Anyone can call a dive at any time, for any reason, with no recrimination. The team must plan for all eventualities.

A training dive should be just that, and must never encompass exploration or other activities. The accompanying instructor or experienced diver must concentrate solely upon the inexperienced diver and not be distracted from this duty by the excitement of the unknown. The lure of exploration may be tempting for both divers, but following this path immediately takes them beyond the parameters of the dive plan.

For an inexperienced diver the aim of the dive should be clear, so that it proceeds from start to finish with no surprises. Divers who deviate from a plan are blatantly irresponsible if their primary aim was to supervise others in their charge. Such people should not be called instructors.

Once individuals and teams move beyond active instruction, they should plan dives with people of similar experience. If a group's cross-section of skills and experience is too great, unseen pressures are likely to be created; an inexperienced diver may feel the need to 'prove' himself, or at the very least attempt not to be the weakest link in the chain. A skilful diver may have forgotten how difficult it was to perform some tasks while less experienced, and may misinterpret an artificially raised level of competence in a recently trained but nevertheless inexperienced diver, thinking that this ability is normal. Strains are inevitable and will eventually cause problems.

Honest, open communication is the key to successful dive planning. Everyone must understand from the outset what the dive plan is; if you are uncertain about anything you have a moral obligation to ask for an explanation. Do not be afraid to 'show yourself up' by asking some seemingly trivial question; if it is nagging you, it must be dealt with. The query may reveal other unseen or unanticipated matters, which may be more important. Such discussion is immensely beneficial to all team members – and it all helps anticipate possible scenarios that might develop during the dive.

Thoroughly consider both likely and unlikely situations. What complications might be induced by the environment; what are the details of equipment, air management, visibility, currents, personnel and stress? All have a bearing upon the safety and outcome of the dive.

Teamwork is needed both in planning and executing the dive – as here in Mexico

With limited visibility and constricted sites at many locations in the UK, diving solo is common. In comparison with sites that are warm and clear, diving as a team is not viable.

This diver is reversing into a tight section of cave, reeling his line out behind him. Divers predominantly used to working alone should refresh communication skills before undertaking projects as part of a team

When you reach a dive site undertake a detailed site inspection and discuss it with the team; the area may have changed and diving might now be impractical or impossible. Before entering the water clarify essential roles: who is the leader? Who will do what and dive in which position? Underwater communication should be reviewed and the dive plan reduced to its simplest form so that it is understood by all. The role of pre-dive communication cannot be overemphasised.

Underwater communication

When diving with a buddy you must be able to communicate essential instructions and information. How much interaction is possible depends on the proficiency of the team and environmental conditions. Divers who are already good friends will have mutual respect and a good foundation to base communication on. Maintaining good communication underwater relies on alertness and response; it starts with 'buddy awareness' and each person should develop the habit of making regular checks of team members.

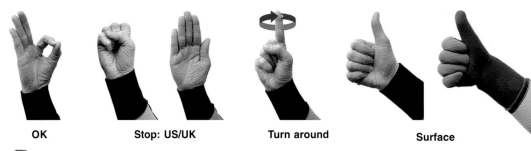

| OK | Stop: US/UK | Turn around | Surface |

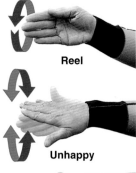

Reel

Unhappy

Line

Make a belay

Entanglement

Hand signals

Agree communication signs before a dive, to avoid confusion. Hand signals differ around the world, in particular 'stop' (a clenched fist in the USA and an open palm in the UK). Other signals may be unfamiliar to a visitor.

Also consider water conditions – though a 'surface' signal is readily identifiable, wearing a glove in poor visibility may render others (such as 'entanglement' – a figure-of-eight movement with crossed fingers) impossible or, at best, extremely difficult to recognise

Communication underwater is often frustrating. A well-planned operation will anticipate probable difficulties and specific signals can be agreed before the dive. In optimum conditions an efficient team normally uses light signals, perhaps backed by hand signals – it is extremely important that everyone understands these.

If the need arises, more complicated information may written on a dive slate; in optimum conditions each diver should keep one instantly accessible. However, handwriting underwater is frequently poor, a problem exacerbated by cold hands and a limited area for writing, plus which it takes time to set the words down. Poor visibility may overrule this option altogether, and pencils can break; using a slate may therefore prove impossible. Sound is limited underwater although it can be used to attract attention – though as technology improves, its use by recreational divers will undoubtedly increase.

A crude but immensely important method of communicating relies on touch. In deteriorating visibility divers must maintain close contact with the line. In a complete silt-out it is reassuring to uphold even limited communication, which of necessity will be via touch. Under the American scheme of cave diving training, low visibility diving has received extensive studies.

Communication methods require prior agreement and whatever system is implemented those signals should be practised – especially those intended for use in zero visibility. The Rimbach system, the bump-and-go or touch-and-go system, and a variant known as the Wilson system, are variously employed. Rimbach signals are 'go forwards', conveyed by pulling or pushing a diver's limb in the onward direction, and 'back up', communicated by pulling or pushing backwards. 'Stop' (stay where you are) is indicated with a single deliberate squeeze. In the USA multiple squeezes convey that assistance is required or that there is an emergency.

These communications are important. They all require prior agreement and understanding before use in what will be a potentially stressful situation. While the aim is to regain visibility at the earliest opportunity, it is important that each diver remains calm. The way that contact is made – the manner of clasping and holding, especially initially – conveys a lot of information about your companion's self-control and mental state. Three controlled, firm but gentle squeezes might communicate that you are not only present, but that you are calm and ready to take appropriate steps to do whatever is required. Receiving a similar response is very reassuring.

Hand signals are commonly used in diving, although the majority are rendered useless if the diver wears thick gloves or the visibility is poor. In clear, warm water such as is found in Florida and Mexico some highly elaborate signals have been devised and here their usefulness is beyond question.

Before diving, discuss the most likely signals you will need: those such as OK, surface, stop, turn around and problem must be clearly understood. Signals vary, in particular those used in Europe and the USA. In the USA a clenched fist indicates stop or hold, for example, while in Britain this requires an upright open palm. In warm water environments a diver's attention can be drawn to the line by crossing the middle finger over the index finger. This, and a multitude of other signals, is wholly impractical in cold water when wearing thick gloves.

In the American cave diving community, where hand-held lights are the norm, scores of signals are made using the other, free hand. However, in comparison, head-mounted lighting leaves both hands free to communicate more expressively (and sometimes less ambiguously). Remember to shine your light on the hand making the signal and not into your buddy's eyes. Divers visiting Florida or similar climes should refer to specialist publications on cave hand signals, which go beyond those used in open water.

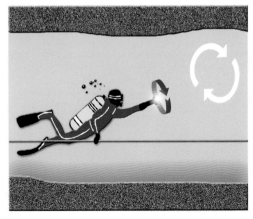

In clear water it may be possible to communicate at a distance. A light moved in a circle signals 'I am okay'; it is also the standard response: 'I am okay'. The motion is easier to create with a hand-held light, but it can also be achieved with a helmet-mounted light. Calm, controlled movement is important; this also conveys a great deal about the well-being of the owner. Rapid movements attract attention, but not if the individual's behaviour has previously been jerky and erratic. Convention has established that vertical flashing indicates urgency while horizontal flashing communicates emergency, but in the confines of a cave or silty wreck these distinctions are best regarded as academic and divers should assume that all vigorous light movements denote urgency or emergency and that the owner requires attention and a response.

Where hand signals cannot be conveniently used, for example when divers are too far apart, communicate 'OK' by shining a light on a wall in a circular pattern

Clear water permits effective communication, but visibility that was perfect at the outset of a dive may be destroyed in moments by poor silt technique or buoyancy control. Other factors beyond the control of the team may have an equivalent effect, such as a sudden rainstorm flushing fine silt into the waterway or another team encountering severe problems of its own. Plan to communicate with other members of your team under *all* conditions.

Checks and drills

All equipment must be checked to ensure that it is serviceable. Thorough in-water, pre-dive drills must be undertaken. Begin with a bubble check to satisfy everyone that there are no gas leaks in the equipment. Lights and regulators follow, then finally accessories. Everything needed on the dive – reels, knives, tables – must be tested and seen to function underwater. The team should compare equipment by matching like with like, and a head-to-toe inspection of each other's kit should pick up potential problems. Solo divers should similarly adhere to a routine set of checks; everything is inspected. Do not be tempted to cut corners because the water is cold. Stick to the plan – stick to your routine.

Perform a Safety or S-drill. Because you have gained certification this does not mean you are excused from this air-sharing exercise. The drill was conceived for a purpose and you were instructed in it for a reason. Breathe from each other's apparatus and swim for a short distance, so that you are fully aware of all the equipment and configurations. You might be grateful for that knowledge later.

Before setting off into the depths ensure that your turnaround

Silt, disturbed by the diver's bubbles, drops from the ceiling in Cenote Dos Pisos, Mexico. Visibility will be poorer on the return dive

pressure is written on your slate, along with the time the dive started and, if appropriate, the compass 'out' bearing. Check your no decompression status and, last but not least, that everyone fully understands and is happy with the proposed dive plan. Remember that this is a recreational activity, not a survival exercise.

Your planning checklist

- Plan the dive carefully, with attention to detail
- Discuss the dive thoroughly, honestly and openly with all team members
- Anticipate all scenarios – the plan must be comprehensive and flexible
- Agree limits, especially turnaround, time, and depth
- Establish contingency plans – for decompression sickness or other emergencies
- Agree communications, especially those for poor visibility
- Complete pre-dive drills
- Before setting off, ensure that everyone is happy and clearly understands the plan

Chapter nine
Techniques

USING an optimum set of equipment in a particular environment is important for both safety and enjoyment, but it must also be used with the appropriate techniques. The demands of the overhead environment are special and particular consideration must be given to movement within it, in particular swimming.

Buoyancy control and trim

When divers cease forward motion they naturally assume a head-up, feet-down attitude; without care, when they move off again their fin strokes direct a blast of water downwards, all too often resulting in a cloud of sediment rising into the surrounding water. This would not matter in open water (other than in a vulnerable location), as it is easy to swim to clearer conditions. However, silt disturbance may be critical in a wreck or deep within a cave.

There is little doubt that loss of visibility due to silt disturbance has contributed to a large number of cave, wreck and mine-related fatalities. It is therefore extremely important that divers pay close attention to buoyancy to ensure that they 'hover' well clear of the floor in a good swimming position. This is termed trim – good trim requires that divers move through the water horizontally, because a horizontal position is streamlined and expends the least energy.

Correct weighting is extremely important in helping to attain good trim – but so is the form of body movement used to propel the diver forwards. Ideally, the force required is directed horizontally behind the diver, not diagonally downward. Provided that the diver keeps well away from walls

The diver in this 1970s photograph taken at Porth yr Ogof, South Wales lacks good trim or buoyancy control and has an inappropriate finning action. This will cause silt disturbance, a problem exacerbated by exhaled air

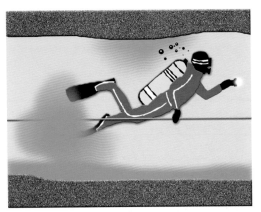

The down-blast from a normal fin stroke disturbs sediment from the floor, while exhaled bubbles may bring down a fine veil of silt from above (the latter problem is minimised when rebreathers are used). The solution is to adopt a horizontal, streamlined swimming position

and floor, there should be minimal silt disturbance from the fin strokes.

Finning techniques have become highly developed by cave divers in Florida. Perhaps the most effective of these is the frog kick, which is similar to the leg action involved in a normal breaststroke. However, skilful divers will employ a variety of strokes, if not specifically due to the nature of the passage, then in order to exercise and rest different leg muscles. The topic is covered in detail in dive manuals published in the USA, and is not covered further here.

Watching a video of yourself diving can be a surprising insight and, together with a supportive, respected buddy prepared to make constructive comments, will provide a valuable learning experience. There is little doubt that once good buoyancy and trim are mastered, dives are much more efficient and enjoyable.

If the current in a tunnel is strong, a decrease in visibility caused by a diver may not be of concern because the sediment cloud is soon carried away. However, kicking up deep, fine silt in a minimal current may be very disturbing and hazardous. It is imperative that the team exercises the utmost caution under these conditions. In general, swimming high in a tunnel keeps divers as far away as possible from the potential problem, as well as minimising depth (therefore aiding air consumption and reducing decompression) and keeping out of the main flow, which normally runs in the middle of the passage.

Low tunnels containing fine sediment must be treated with great

As here in the Gran Cenote system, Mexico, good technique and swimming well above the floor will maintain the best visibility

caution and are best avoided by inexperienced divers until they are comfortable in blackout conditions. Move slowly with careful, minimal finning. To reduce silt disturbance, stop finning for a while and use your hands. A simple breaststroke action using hands alone can be highly effective in passing short sections, providing you have good buoyancy control and trim.

Occasionally, perhaps through lack of anticipation, a diver will accidentally descend towards the silt; what is coming and what you should have done some seconds before is imme-diately obvious, but it is too late. You need to gain height and your first thought is to make a strong fin stroke – but this is not the best solution. With just a metre or so to go and contact inevitable, make no swimming movements at all and 'land' on a gently outstretched hand, which will minimise your impact on the silt, then inflate your buoyancy compensa-tor and wait for positive buoyancy to lift you clear (and be ready to coun-ter the excess buoyancy).

Demonstrating good trim while making a jump in a Mexican cenote

In high flow and a variety of other conditions a 'pull-and-glide' tech-nique, where you ease forward using handholds on the wall or floor, is very effective. The 'ceiling push-off', where the diver does not fin prop-erly but instead uses them to shuffle forward on the ceiling, is also use-ful. However, consider the environmental impact before employing this technique – it would be wholly inappropriate in the well-decorated caves of Mexico's Yucatán peninsula.

There is little doubt that in the large clear springs of Florida and Mexico, diving is akin to flight. Gliding effortlessly through superbly sculpted and fabulously adorned cave passages is a wonderful, magnificent experience. To lose visibility in such a setting is an indescribable loss; enjoyment is quickly replaced by concern and anguish. Bad techniques that raise sediment severely detract from the team's enjoyment and may signal the end of the dive, plus which there could be several other teams in the vicinity at a popular site – and you will not be thanked for spoiling their day.

It often surprises and disturbs cave divers from Florida when they learn that some European cave divers are prepared to dive without finely ad-justed buoyancy or trim. Controlling a diver's position in the water is not of prime importance where passages may be restricted and diving deep underground is conducted solo. Such divers may be forced to squeeze through banks of silt and of necessity combat cold water and extremely poor visibility. There is a good reason for such an approach, normally because the environment precludes the safe addition of bulky extra equip-ment. Dives may exceed a couple of hours and many highly sophisticated techniques and approaches may be employed. In every respect the commitment of these divers speaks for itself.

One technique that has been refined by Europeans is what Florida divers refer to as 'line and environmental awareness'. When visibility is good and divers can follow a line without holding it, they maintain a heightened sense of line awareness to ensure that they always know its

Haloclines greatly impair visibility, as seen in this Menorcan cave. Selecting good belay points and effective line laying are important in such areas

position and the exit direction. The guideline should always be within easy reach. Referencing is closely associated, where the diver absorbs as much information about the surroundings as possible; it is a memory exercise conducted on the way in while water clarity is at its best, logging details such as line belay points, line traps and junctions. There may be zero visibility on the return dive, during which a good memory will help immeasurably.

A diver's primary navigational aid is always the line, but referencing is an extremely valuable supplementary technique. The skill takes considerable experience to acquire, but the process generally accelerates when the novice begins to lead rather than follow the fins of other members of the group.

Low visibility diving

There are two main forms of low visibility. The first occurs naturally due to suspended particles, pollution, tannic acid, peat staining, haloclines or rainfall run-off; the second is best described as incidental low visibility caused by diver-induced silting and other human and equipment failures. Where these conditions are prevalent or predictable, dives must be planned and undertaken with infinitely greater care.

Communication in low visibility is more problematic and while buddy diving may remain possible, its benefits must be closely weighed. It is essential that each diver is completely self-reliant and, if conditions deteriorate, it may be prudent for the 'second' diver to withdraw. At the outset, low visibility diving projects must be planned as potential solo operations. In a constricted site with bad visibility it is nearly always better to dive solo, as having two people stir up silt is much worse than one.

Maintaining close contact and being able to feel the line, especially when wearing gloves, is essential, so in poor conditions the line should be at least 3mm thick. In addition, it should be belayed carefully and with greater frequency, and followed more slowly than usual. Using the walls and/or the floor (not the line) to pull on, gliding forward, is a favoured technique to minimise silt disturbance.

Dark-coloured neoprene is extremely difficult to distinguish in low light, even half a metre away. Adding reflective material such as silver tape to fins, cylinders and suits will help other divers to see you and this reduces the likelihood of accidental collision with a buddy. If a collision should occur, wearing a helmet helps to prevent mask displacement.

Diving in low visibility exerts a more intense psychological strain on a diver than when exploring large, clear passages. This is an important consideration for those who have trained in the clear springs of Florida or Mexico.

Chapter ten
Emergencies

No matter how experienced the diver, no matter how thorough the preparations or how limited the objective, a critical situation can still arise. A relatively minor problem for an experienced diver may become an emergency for the inexperienced. For relatively inexperienced divers, therefore, their level of training should dictate the selection of appropriate diving sites. Specifically, they should not subject themselves to situations that experienced divers might consider unduly rash.

It is often said that cave diving is easy, until something goes wrong – and it is only then that the effectiveness of training comes into its own. Skills learned in those early days must be thoroughly ingrained by repeated practice and, in the same manner, emergency techniques must be over-learned (see p72) and become second nature if they are to be relied upon under stress.

The first and most important strategy in a potentially high stress situation is prevention – prevent the problem becoming an emergency by having adequate training, a good dive plan and sticking to it.

Approaches to cavern, cave and overhead environment diving differ substantially around the world. In Europe cave diving is frequently undertaken solo, while in Florida a three-man team is common. Divers train differently for the respective environments and this is reflected in their strategies for problem-solving and emergencies.

Consider what you will do in the event of an accident. First aid kits will deal with cuts and scratches; for more critical problems an oxygen resuscitation set may be required. Establish an emergency procedure; all divers should be aware of the location of, and the telephone number for, the nearest decompression chamber

Loss of visibility

Depending upon the location, training and experience of the diver, a loss of visibility may not be a problem, but to a novice it might be the prelude to an emergency. The diver's primary sense – sight – is greatly impaired and in some cases not even the outline of the passage, other divers or instruments can be seen; everything must be done by touch. In a team a loss of visibility can be a major problem, especially if the line is thin or poorly laid. It is important to remain calm and reassure your companions that you are okay. The group will hopefully leave the area without further delay and review the situation after the dive.

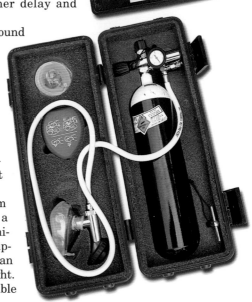

Solo cave divers in the UK have training and background experience which makes them comfortable with being alone in such a predicament; to them, a second person is another source of worry. Solo divers can concentrate totally upon the task in hand.

Light failure

A primary light failure will generate a minor problem for any diver, until the back-up light is activated. The advent of 'long-burn' LED lights will help to alleviate this problem as these can be left on throughout the dive.

Orientation to the guideline is critical until the team is aware of the difficulty. In a well-honed buddy team a companion will be on hand to provide welcome illumination and a sense of direction, but without such support there is little doubt that most back-up lights can be, and generally are, grossly inferior to the primary light. When the switch is made, eyes can take a considerable time to become accustomed to the reduced level.

With a major emphasis on avoiding contact with the floor and ceiling, it is extremely important that a sense of direction is not lost by a solo diver. Loss of a team member's main light normally signals a return to the entrance, with the diver on reserve either repositioned to lead or placed in front of someone using a primary light. With the differing approach taken in British caves or mines, a light failure such as this would pose relatively little difficulty, as divers routinely use two or even four head-mounted lights at the same time.

Entanglement

Both a loss of visibility and primary light failure are problematic, but entanglement is more serious. A solo diver must remain calm, stop and think, then respond according to the line position in the passage and the

Loose line (especially loose floating line) can easily cause entanglement. Here, line has caught upon a diver's fin strap, fortunately in an area free of silt

nature of the site. In smaller tunnels, certainly in Europe and other cold water areas, the diver will normally settle quietly on the floor to gain a stable position and retain a sense of direction, though in a large tunnel it may be prudent to move to the ceiling, especially if there is light silt present. Depending upon how and where the line was laid this may not be possible, as it is important not to pull upon or stress the line.

Once stable, the diver can establish the manner of entanglement and, in the majority of cases where the line is relatively thick, rectify the problem fairly quickly. Providing the diver is inside 'Thirds' (has not used more than one-third of the available air) and the only problems are entanglement and visibility loss, stopping for a moment should not cause excessive stress. The benefits of stopping and regaining composure cannot be overemphasised. After freeing the entanglement the diver can exit, leaving the line to be rebelayed or repositioned on a later occasion.

Entanglement in thin line is serious and must be handled quickly and efficiently. Depending upon the environment, a buddy's assistance is invaluable. The entangled diver should strive to avoid further movement, which is likely to make matters worse, and hold the 'out' line while a companion does whatever is required. Providing the buddy is on hand before effective visibility is lost, he or she can probably determine the cause of the problem far more easily than a trapped diver. Avoiding further deterioration in visibility is important, so the team should try to stay clear of the floor.

If time or other factors are critical, the line may need to be cut, but this should only be considered in the direst of emergencies. Place team members on the safe 'out' side of the entanglement before cutting, while holding firmly to the correct half of the line without pulling on it. Ideally, a repair should then be made using a gap reel, if available air and the diver's mental state permit.

Out of air

Out-of-air situations should never arise if the supply has been carefully managed, but associated emergencies do occur. Assuming the Rule of Thirds is strictly adhered to the diver should be able to address the crisis; experienced, suitably equipped divers will stand a much better chance

Minor problems may become exacerbated by elements of the overhead environment. A constricted exit from a cave or wreck, for example, could add to difficulties if the diver is already short of air

of survival. Again, training and experience are the crux of the matter.

A solo diver with independent single cylinders should have sufficient air to exit on one alone, provided the diver remains calm. If air is being lost due to a severe leak, the failing supply should be used first. Wearing a side-mounted system makes it reassuringly easy to open and close the cylinder valve when required, to permit breathing. Being able to isolate and regulate air in this manner is extremely important as, unless they are shut down promptly, modern regulators can empty a cylinder in a matter of minutes.

Reaching cylinder valves and/or a manifold isolator on the diver's back is more awkward and, with the potentially vulnerable valve connections lying outside the field of vision, it takes longer to identify the nature of an air emergency. Wearing a bulky drysuit may also compromise your ability to access and tackle the problem, but if you are on your own you must be able to address all matters without delay.

A total air failure is extremely rare, but it is worth training for this eventuality in a team situation. How far can you swim in full kit in an emergency, having already exhaled? As this is not far, buddies must re-main close at hand and both divers must know which regulator to use in an emergency. Here, opinions differ – some advocate that the out-of-air diver uses the regulator in the donor's mouth (which means that the stricken diver knows that it is fully functional, but the potential surprise may be stressful for the donor), while others prefer that the out-of-air diver goes directly to the reserve.

Divers should plan and undertake an S-drill to prepare for a sudden, total air loss (if a diver runs low on air there should be no delay in alert-ing others, before the situation becomes critical). Ideally, as soon as an out-of-air signal is received the donor will be immediately fully primed to pass over a reserve. The process must be as stress-free as possible.

Other than in the most spacious of tunnels, buddy breathing while swimming out from an overhead environment is best undertaken using a long hose. Most Americans breathe from a long hose – a 1.5m hose is regarded as minimal; a 2m hose is preferred in Florida. Even so, the potential for losing visibility is greatly increased while sharing air and the long hose must be handled with care. Undue stress at the first stage connection could cause a rupture, which would be catastrophic. Experi-ence indicates that the out-of-air diver should exit in front of the donor.

Laying line is imperative at all sites. This diver in the Medas Islands, Spain, is carrying a small reel, but has not yet belayed it

Lost diver

If a diver becomes lost this is potentially the most critical emergency possible. Much depends on the meaning of 'lost', but in all probability any lost diver will be stressed and breathing more rapidly. With dwindling air reserves and a preoccupation with finding the line, other requirements such as silt control and environmental awareness are rapidly overruled.

It is possible, though very rare, to completely lose your sense of direction, even while following a fixed line. Zero current, poor visibility or some distraction (for example, mask clearing) that causes a momentary release of the line, can all contribute to disorientation. Losing orientation is extremely unlikely when diving as part of a team, unless some serious navigational error has been made. In the event of uncertainty, divers must look for line markers, silt markings on the floor and any observable current. If the geographical layout of the system is relatively straightforward, and the diver remembers details of the survey (and has an out-bearing on a slate), a compass is invaluable. Experience with a compass is needed before a diver will fully trust it while stressed, when rational thought may be difficult and sight is limited.

If someone in a team is missing, this is normally due to loss of visibility or a problem that caused the diver to lose the line. If visibility is poor, it will probably soon become worse and finding the diver quickly is essential – the longer a diver is off-line the greater the level of anxiety, so be prepared to give immediate assistance and reassurance when the diver is found.

When searching, shield your own light to help look for a light source away from the line; if this is seen, slowly sweep your own light across the tunnel as a signal. Continue to monitor your own air reserves and remember that, in worsening visibility, gauges may become unreadable and this, coupled with the stress of the search, may increase breathing rates for all team members. Moving a few metres along the line may gain clearer water and reduce stress, as well as allowing you to see the lost diver's light.

If it is suspected that the lost diver has accidentally entered a side route, or is lost some distance from the line, an experienced diver with ample reserves might make a search by attaching a safety reel to the main line in the same manner as when making a jump. Before reeling out, an 'out' arrow or clothes peg should be placed on the 'safe' side of the T-junction in the line. Assuming that the diver is found, present a calm attitude then position the diver in front to lead the way out. Reaching the 'out' line marker will provide reassurance of the correct direction to the surface.

Inevitably, if the diver is not found, the point arrives when you must exit. The timing of this decision is difficult, but you must not jeopardise the safety of others for a diver who may already be beyond help or has possibly relocated the line and is already en route to the exit.

If you become lost the most important thing to do is stop and compose yourself. As soon as you lose the line take a couple of deliberate, calming breaths and hold position. If you move off blindly looking for the line or your companions, the chances are that you will move deeper into trouble. Remaining stationary, even if this means carefully putting a stabilising fin on the floor, is essential. Think about what led to the loss of line: might it only be an arm's length away, or was it broken? What type, size and colour is it? Where is the line laid in the passage, and what is the passage like? With composure, you can hopefully derive additional clues from the environment that might help solve your problem. Did you leave a silt trail? Which way is the current flowing? Think.

Hopefully, using a safety reel will not be required. As with all skills,

Search and recover

There are many scenarios which might cause a diver to lose the line. The first action in any such emergency is to drop a weight to fix position and use a safety reel (see p91) to make a slow, methodical search in a horizontal plane. There are no guarantees that this will succeed, as in this plan diagram where the line has drifted into a line trap.

With sufficient line on the safety reel it may be possible to extend the search area and locate the lost line beyond the boulders. Remaining calm is essential. If this extended search also fails there is no option but to move down the passage to conduct a second search, using whatever aids are available to help determine the direction to take (such as following a wall). Here, hopefully, the passage configuration differs and, using the new anchor position, the line can be located

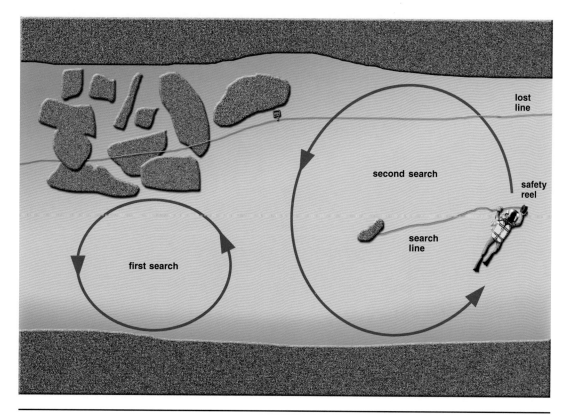

Careful line laying in
El Moraig on Spain's
Costa Blanca

you will only feel confident about using it if you have thoroughly practised lost line drills. In a team situation your companions should quickly realise that you are not with them, and begin a search. Shield your light against your chest and look for the glow of their lights. If this fails sweep your light from side to side in the direction from which you came to attract attention. Keep thinking.

For a solo diver operating in a typical British environment (or a team diver who has not been found), relocating a 'lost line' requires a positive mental attitude. The need for composure and a stationary position cannot be stressed too highly. Both will reduce further silt disturbance and help to maintain a sense of direction. Contact with the floor is normally required if this is to be effective. From this position the diver can slowly sweep the nearby available space to feel for the line and only if this fails is the safety reel put to use.

A small weight (preferably already attached to the reel) is dropped and anchored as securely as the environment permits; a handy snoopy loop may prove invaluable as it could be at-

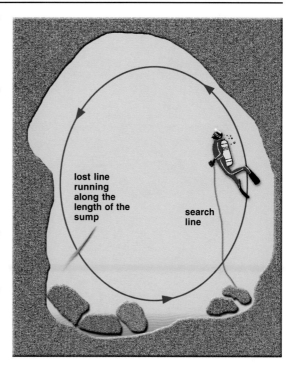

lost line running along the length of the sump

search line

tached to a stone. If the tunnel floor is fairly flat a slow, methodical search is then made across it from wall to wall, perhaps in a circle. As long as the line was laid fairly low in the tunnel and is regularly belayed, the wall-to-wall pattern is likely to locate it, and is therefore preferred as a first measure.

If the line is not found, search by swimming around the circumference of the passage. This presents some difficulties in circumnavigation, especially if the passage is more than a few metres in diameter. In larger, flat-roofed tunnels, such as mines, there is a danger that you may lose your direction and track along the roof rather than correctly across it. However, if the complete cross-section search can be achieved, returning to rest on the floor once again, the lost line can be recovered by carefully winding the search line back onto its reel (assuming that the main line is still intact) and you will soon be safely on your way out once more.

In the Americas, divers rely upon tying a safety line to a rock, wall projection or some other object (perhaps a back-up light) as an anchor for the safety reel. In the lavishly decorated tunnels of the Yucatán in Mexico, for example, there is normally no shortage of anchor points, but the passage may be very complex. Here, it is generally considered that a lost diver should lay line from a safety reel for a limited distance using 'gut feeling' as to the right direction. If this first attempt fails, the diver then winds in the line back to the belay and moves out at a different angle to try again. Such an approach reduces the chance of the diver accidentally relocating his own safety line and becoming confused; having a different coloured line from the main guideline on the safety reel (perhaps pink or yellow) will almost certainly remove this concern.

A broken or severed line is more worrying. A diver arriving at the frayed end of a line might find no sign of the other part. In Britain, where flood damage to permanent line is a constant concern, main line belays should be made at least every 10m, preferably on the floor and close against one wall, to limit the potential gap. The limited amount of line on the safety reel should then be sufficient to bridge the gap and save the day. In the

A vertical search

If the first search, made on the floor of the sump, fails to locate the lost line, conduct a vertical search by swimming up the wall, across the roof to descend the far wall and return to the start point. The search line should trap and regain the lost line.

It is possible, given poor visibility, to swim up the wall and then lose orientation at roof level – after which the diver swims along the roof next to the wall, descends and returns to the start point without having left the same side of the sump. If a vertical search fails to trap the line, this could be the reason – it is a deceptively easy mistake to make. Repeat the search at ninety degrees from the first; in poor visibility where stress takes its toll and reading a compass may not be possible, the diver will have to guess at a new and better direction to take

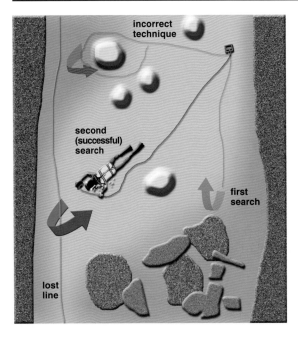

incorrect technique

second (successful) search

first search

lost line

absence of regular line belays, and assisted by a current, it is possible for the severed end to drift some distance away, certainly beyond the limited length of line on the safety reel. This situation is a major concern if the permanent line is made of polypropylene, which floats and will undoubtedly float downstream.

Locating a thin line in cold water or poor visibility is very difficult, especially using gloved hands. When the visibility is bad concentrate upon remaining calm and move very slowly on the search. Any fast movement with a sweeping hand may cause a loose or severed main line to waft further away.

Everything in a real life lost-line emergency is enormously stressful; if it is to be conducted effectively, search training must be practised thoroughly in a safe or supervised environment. Only with practice, and previous success in this endeavour, will a diver feel capable of deploying a safety reel with any confidence.

Out-and-back searches

A technique used in the Americas to relocate a lost line is to make multiple out-and-back searches using a safety line from an anchor point. If a continuous search is made there is a risk of swimming around an obstacle such as a stalagmite and linking back onto the search line (the upper search in this diagram). Instead, the diver swims until reaching an obstacle, then reels back in before heading out again on a new bearing. Here, the first search was unsuccessful and the diver turned back at the boulders, but the second search located the lost line

Depth

Depth can generate its own emergencies which, by definition, are equal to if not more critical than those already described. The advice is clear: gain experience slowly in water of 40m depth or less. Narcotic impairment has occurred in shallower waters than 30m and this experience, in combination with rapidly diminishing air reserves and poor visibility, is not pleasurable. Avoid excessive depth and progressively and slowly acclimatise to deeper dives, perhaps using helium to ensure a clear head.

In conclusion, anticipating problems is something all divers should think about. Pre-dive preparation is crucial. Over-learning skills and their maintenance cannot be emphasised enough. Composure and the ability to think clearly are paramount when an emergency arises.

In an emergency
- Stop and take two or three good controlled breaths
- Regain mental control
- Think the problem through to the most appropriate solution
- Act as you were trained
- Evaluate – has the problem been solved?

Chapter eleven
Advanced Techniques

THUS far this book has concerned itself with the basics of diving in the overhead environment. Moving beyond these techniques requires considerable thought, even greater preparation and, most importantly, additional training. This chapter presents a brief overview of some of the facets inherent in advanced technical diving.

Scooters

Growing numbers of recreational and exploratory divers use scooters (also known as diver propulsion vehicles: DPV) to further their interests. Well over twenty per cent of cave divers in the USA own one or more scooters and there can be little dispute that using one to tour a cave or mine is thoroughly enjoyable. Apart from this a scooter is normally used to

extend a diver's range. However affluent you are, though, it is essential to consider and reflect upon the possible advantages and pitfalls of using a mechanical means of propulsion.

Before using a scooter in an overhead environment the diver must already be thoroughly competent and experienced in that domain. Scooters can travel at several times the speed permitted by finning, at perhaps 50m per minute or more compared with 20m by fin power. Because the unit makes relatively little physical demand upon the diver, significantly less gas is consumed compared with swimming.

Potential problems include collisions with the cave, the greater likelihood of silting and mechanical failure. Failure may be caused by battery discharge, poor battery charging, water ingress or a fouled propeller. To avoid fouling it is essential that equipment carried on the scooter is neatly

Two divers with scooters about to enter the crystal clear waters of Little River Springs, Florida

The long-distance scooter used by Rick Stanton, a renowned British cave diving pioneer, prepared for an exploratory dive. Scooters drastically increase the effective range that a diver can attain

Transporting a scooter to a remote underground site may present problems. A small scooter may therefore be more practical, as here in Noxon Park Iron Mine

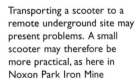

and well secured so that it cannot be sucked into the propeller. Helmets are recommended, not only as protection from direct contact with the rock, but also to serve as an alternative place to mount primary lights, which also leaves hands free for other tasks.

The prime consideration is redundancy. If you intend to venture a long way into a tunnel are you physically equipped and mentally prepared to make an unassisted exit by fin power? In caves and mines you should not scooter into unfamiliar passage; take the scooter to the furthest point you have previously finned to, drop it off and continue swimming under your own power. On the next dive scooter to the new maximum limit, exploring via progressive penetrations. This procedure allows the explorer to become familiar with the passage, the flow, the positioning and condition of the line, and to check on gas management.

Gas management when using scooters must be more conservative than when swimming. Addressing the worse case scenario, the diver must determine how much gas is required to swim out from the furthest point. Each site must be carefully considered according to passage size, visibility, depth, flow and obstacles. A Rule of Sixths is safest, certainly at the outset. Depending on the objective and the team's ability to conduct a rescue from the furthest limits, a Rule of Fourths might be acceptable. On committing dives the 'how to get out' requirement might be addressed by placing safety bottles en route, or carrying other redundancy.

When on a scooter the diver's overall awareness must be raised above normal because everything happens at a much faster pace. Individuals must be able to navigate the way home and, if diving as a team, line and environmental awareness, buddy awareness and assistance are essential. The team must be able to react to a problem quickly and efficiently.

Likewise, its members must be capable of incorporating the scooter into their rescue or emergency procedures.

A scooter checklist
Using a scooter is certainly beneficial, but only in the hands of a trained diver with the right attitude.

Ensure that you:
- Are thoroughly competent and experienced in the particular overhead environment before using a scooter
- Know how the scooter functions and how to maintain it
- Have trained with the scooter in open water
- Pay special care to environmental orientation – everything happens much faster
- Carefully consider buddy awareness, assistance and rescue scenarios
- Practise rescue skills in open water; be able to share air while diving and tow a disabled scooter and/or diver for a distance equivalent to the maximum planned penetration
- Use an appropriate (conservative) gas consumption rule, perhaps one-sixth
- Only use the scooter for progressive penetrations

Other gases
As part of recreational and exploratory diving, it is becoming commoner to use gases other than compressed air. When used appropriately, gas mixtures can improve a dive's safety margin by reducing the risk of:

- Narcosis
- Decompression liability
- Oxygen toxicity

Nitrox is a breathable mixture of variable composition involving a reduced amount of nitrogen and a higher proportion of oxygen than in normal air. Diving on elevated levels of oxygen means less exposure to nitrogen, which reduces the risk of nitrogen narcosis and significantly aids decompression, not to mention an improved well-being after the dive. Note, though, the effects of oxygen on the body are increased – see p60. However, the foremost concern is that, although using nitrox can be immensely beneficial at depths of between 20m and 40m, when diving deeper the advantages diminish and the element of danger increases. To ignore this or be casual towards nitrox is grossly irresponsible; you risk oxygen convulsion and drowning, which may occur with little or no warning.

South American diver Gilberto Menezes shows an array of equipment used for a solo dive to 90m depth in Formoso Springs, Bonito, Brazil

The maximum operating depth (MOD) for a particular nitrox mixture is determined by the percentage of oxygen it contains, which relates to the partial pressure that the diver is exposed to at the maximum depth. Below 40m other blends of mixed gas play a role. To reduce the nitrogen content and risk of narcosis, helium is added to the mix. This may involve removing or completely eliminating nitrogen from the breathing supply, while also possibly reducing the oxygen content.

Helium is the least narcotic of the inert gases. It may be included in the cylinder along with oxygen and nitrogen to form trimix; with oxygen alone the mixture is termed heliox. It is possible (and frequently more practical on expeditions) to partially fill cylinders with helium and then top them up with air. This mixture is termed heliair.

While helium is acknowledged for its benefits at depth, where it is light and easier to breathe than air, it has particularly low insulating capabilities and carries heat away from the body more rapidly than air. As a consequence, helium mixtures should not be used for drysuit inflation, a function best fulfilled by using a small, dedicated bottle of argon.

Pat Cronin double-checking the contents of a diving cylinder using a gas analyser. This precaution gives peace of mind prior to a deep dive

Mixed gas diving is a complex area of study, where understanding is still evolving. Knowledge of partial pressures is important in every stage of diving, but working with mixed gases requires attention to formulae and tables while submerging in detailed technicalities. Computers and gas analysers can assist dive planning, although divers must have a complete understanding of the rationale behind these aids – for example, body tissues absorb helium faster than nitrogen and special tables or computer models are therefore required to determine decompression times. Acronyms such as END (Equivalent Narcotic Depth), CNS (Central Nervous System) toxicity, OTUs (Oxygen Tolerance Units) and others become part of calculations. Mixed gas dives must be planned with great care and executed with even greater precision than those in shallow water.

A variety of pre-dive decisions must be made. One of the most important is the optimum level of narcotic exposure (END), which is influenced not only by physiological factors but also by the availability and cost of helium. Working through set procedures, familiarity with gas fractions is gained and divers can then determine the most appropriate one to use for dives on an individual basis.

When filling a cylinder the dive shop will require certification; once filled the cylinder is analysed for content and labelled, after which any responsible, safety-conscious diver will check the mix (oxygen content is critical in determining the MOD) before signing for the gas, absolving the shop from liability. The normal convention is to show the percentage of oxygen first, helium second and nitrogen last. As an example, a diver might have a 16–40–44 trimix for a dive to 79m, and dive or computer-generated tables will present essential decompression obligation information.

Decompression can be made safer by using one or more nitrox mixes during the final stage of the dive, which entails considerable financial outlay for cylinders and regulators that must be kept oxygen clean and are effectively dedicated to deep diving projects. The cost of mixed gas diving is significantly greater than that incurred by normal recreational diving. For in-depth coverage of technical diving refer to *Technical Diving from the Bottom Up* by Kevin Gurr.

Rebreathers

Rebreather technology has an extremely valuable role to play in overhead environment diving. The design principle pre-dates open circuit technology, but only today is the climate right for its commercial production for recreational diving. The modern generation of rebreathers has been manufactured to the highest standards, though it is equally apparent

Front and rear views of a Halcyon semi-closed rebreather, set up and ready for use at the Émergence du Ressel, France in 1999 (left), and preparing for a training dive using a Draeger semi-closed rebreather at Porth yr Ogof, South Wales (below)

that they must be operated with a clinical attention to care and detail. A 'rebreather mindset' is essential.

Diving on air – using open circuit equipment – a diver breathes 79% nitrogen and 21% oxygen. The body requires only about 4% of the air breathed for metabolism (dropping the oxygen content to 17%) and some 96% of each breath is vented into the water. At 90m depth (10 bar), even though the diver's consumption of gas is ten times greater than on the surface, the same amount of oxygen is used. Regardless of depth the body will only metabolise the same proportion of oxygen – about 1 litre per minute – and therefore the amount of wasted gas increases with depth while at the same time depleting reserves and shortening the dive.

A rebreather wastes little or no gas. After breathing, the inert gas component remains in the apparatus and is replenished with oxygen from a reserve (according to the type of rebreather), while a chemical absorbent removes the by-product, carbon dioxide. A 3 litre cylinder of oxygen pressurised to 200 bar contains 600 litres of gas, which could maintain a diver underwater for some 600 minutes, irrespective of the depth. Compared with open circuit equipment, gas consumption is minute and less has to be carried.

There are other benefits to be derived from a rebreather. The chemical reaction involved with the absorption of carbon dioxide generates heat, which keeps the diver significantly warmer than when breathing from an open circuit supply that delivers its gas at water temperature. Additionally, an open circuit apparatus dehydrates the diver because the inhaled supply is dry but the exhaled gas is moist, having picked up water from the lungs. A rebreather, however, retains any moisture within the breathing loop. Remaining warm and suitably hydrated are important

A support diver assists rebreather diver Jill Heinerth (left), prior to a mission into Wakulla Springs

factors in preventing decompression sickness. Additionally, few or no exhaust bubbles are produced and this means that silt disturbance from a passage roof is less likely.

Rebreathers are classified into two types: semi-closed (SCR) and fully closed (CCR). Semi-closed rebreathers are less complicated and generally less expensive than their counterparts, but normally do not have as great a duration. Fully closed rebreathers place a heavy reliance upon electronics and oxygen sensors, which can be prone to malfunction. Redundancy is a key area in rebreather technology and different models offer varying protection. In the event of an electronics failure, the best CCR rebreathers allow the diver to switch to a semi-closed state, providing time to exit.

There are a growing number of rebreathers on the market, some better suited than others for enclosed environments. Divers drawn toward this technology must consider what they are aiming to achieve. There are obvious exciting applications for explorers and photographers alike, but neither rebreathers nor mixed gas will ever render the use of air obsolete. Each is but a means to an end – a tool to be used as and when appropriate.

Conclusion

Before contemplating mixed gas or any other form of advanced or technical diving in caves, mines or wrecks, it is essential that all divers are completely at home in this environment. There are sound reasons why cavern and cave diving programmes have been structured the way they are and divers should reflect carefully before progressing from one level to the next.

Environmental awareness is essential to properly exercise the techniques and equipment that blend into a formula for underwater safety. 'Combining the planning, methodology, equipment and teamwork that comprise a safe and enjoyable cave dive takes much practise.' (NACD)

Chapter twelve
A Final Comment

DIVERS travel widely to experience different environments. While they may gain considerable experience in one sphere of the overhead environment, it must not be taken as read that such a level of competence can immediately be transferred to another. There is a world of difference between diving in the cold, murky waters of northern Europe – whether in sumps, wrecks or below ice – and the warm, clear springs of Florida or Mexico. It is not a question of one area requiring more advanced diving, but that environmental differences must be treated with respect and caution. A diver trained and certified in one region should plan carefully and redress any shortcomings before undertaking an ambitious project in another.

Every diver – whether cave, wreck or mine orientated – has a responsibility to the wider diving community. Specifically, divers should never act unsafely or jeopardise relationships with landowners or local authorities. This is a contentious subject, but the reality is clear: any incident, whether it involves injury or fatality, inconsiderate vehicle parking or changing, dropping litter or using loud or bad language, can result in a site being closed. It can take years to establish good relationships with a landowner, but minutes to lose it all!

Further, divers must never forget that we owe an overwhelming responsibility to the environment. In the fabulous blue holes of the Bahamas or the wonderfully decorated systems of Mexico's Yucatán,

Cave Divers Association of Australia students at Mount Gambier attending a Penetration Diver Course briefing. This is the highest level of cave diving certification in the country

the need for conservation is obvious – but the same care and consideration is required at every site, including caves prone to severe, forceful flooding which may therefore not carry any decorations. Please reflect that mines should also be respected; there is nothing more distasteful than finding scattered rubbish at a dive site.

Diving communities around the world understand that there are many reasons for entering a submerged cave, diving beneath ice or penetrating a wreck, besides those linked to recreation. Apart from exploration at the frontier of the sport, divers are involved with scientific studies – hydrology, geology, biology and archaeology, to name a few – and others wish to film or photograph. It is accepted that these are perfectly legitimate reasons for being in the overhead environment, but it is equally important that everyone – whatever their motives – follows the same tenets of accepted practice as are used by those experienced in the field.

Active cave diving instructors are an excellent resource for training and information. Undertaking a specialist course, making personal contact with those involved, is infinitely preferable to reading a publication. Instead of taking an equipment configuration or diving technique at face value, a couple of minutes of advice may save hours of frustration, not to mention the potential for seriously misinterpreting a written statement. Your selected trainer should be experienced in the sphere of overhead

Given the huge increase in the numbers of divers visiting the fabulous cenotes of Mexico's Yucatán peninsula, the installation of Stop signs (as here, in Gran Cenote) is a highly effective deterrent for inexperienced divers

environment diving that interests you. Then, having discussed your diving in person, it is very reassuring to know that you are going about things the right way.

Basic certification should not mark the end of a diver's training. An increasing number of speciality programmes exist – for example, courses on extended range, mixed gas, rebreathers and scooters – to help divers extend their sphere of diving in as safe a manner as possible. The most important point is that new and varying approaches should be assimilated gradually – even though you may be an intelligent and skilled practitioner, do not attempt to gain your experience in a rush. Take time to consolidate skills before progressing; regularly practise your techniques. Though you were good at something a year ago, it does not mean that you are able to do it now. Training is a never ending-process and you should remain receptive to new ideas and updated equipment.

A student on a cavern diving course prepares to lay line in the resurgence at Porth yr Ogof, South Wales

How should divers prepare themselves for training? Should some be deterred from entering caves or mines? Can trainers do anything to screen their charges; are some psychological profiles unsuited? Or can they help, finding ways to assist novice divers to overcome pressure, from whatever source, to undertake dives that they are not ready for – and may never be ready for? These questions, and others, must be carefully considered by divers at all levels of ability and, in particular, by instructors. Be honest with yourself and before every dive ask: 'Am I capable of self-rescue? Am I capable of buddy rescue in this environment?'

Accident analysis clearly indicates the causes of cave diving fatalities: problems or deficiencies with training, guidelines, air management, depth and lights. Training is at the forefront of combating these factors, certainly for newcomers to the overhead environment, but training alone cannot eliminate all risk; it is only a tool to increase awareness and skills. As in any form of diving (or any sport), experience is invaluable when attaining a competent level of performance. It develops awareness and in so doing contributes to safety. However, even if equipment is sound and the diver is experienced and uses recommended techniques, the human factor remains. In a disturbing number of incidents it appears that errors of judgement have been induced by overconfidence and complacency, something against which we must all guard.

There is absolutely no substitute for a good mental attitude and experience – commonly used terms – to create safe diving conditions in this environment. But what constitutes an experienced diver? Some equate it to the number of years spent partaking in the sport, others to the number of dives undertaken, the variety of dives or perhaps the certifications gained. Yes, these are all a measure of experience, but what really counts is the diver's ability to function effectively when things go seriously wrong. Overhead environment diving is a wonderful experience but it demands extreme respect. Remember: we can all make mistakes.

For a trainee diver, experiencing the wonder of Gran Cenote, near Tulum in Mexico, is something never to be forgotten

Starting out, brushing up
- Undertake a specialist training course
- Some skills are essential: gain them
- Regularly practise your skills
- You cannot rush experience
- Cultivate the right attitude on every dive
- Objectively assess risks on all dives
- Do not exceed your comfort zone
- Take advice, listen to respected divers and structure your development accordingly
- Respect the environment and avoid complacency at all costs

Appendix A
Further Reading

THERE is considerable crossover in overhead environment coverage and, in particular, references for cavern and cave diving are also applicable to wreck and ice diving

General/Technical

United States Navy Diving Manual
DEFENSE DEPT, US NAVY. 5 vols, Rev. (4), US Navy, Washington (1999)

Diving and Subaquatic Medicine
EDMONDS, C., LOWRY, C., PENNEFATHER, J. & WALKER, R. 4th edn, Hodder Arnold, London (2002)

The Darkness Beckons
FARR, MARTYN. 2nd edn, Diadem, London (1991); 3rd edn postscript (2000)

The Technical Diving Handbook
GENTILE, GARY. GGP, Philadelphia (1998)

The Cenotes of the Riviera Maya
GERRARD, STEVE. Puerto Aventuras, Quintana Roo (2000)

Deep Diving
GILLIAM, BRET, VON MAIER, ROBERT & CREA, JOHN. Watersport, San Diego (1995)

Technical Diving from the Bottom Up
GURR, KEVIN. Phoenix Oceaneering, Poole (2002)

Solo Diving
VON MAIER, ROBERT. Watersport, San Diego (1993)

Mixed Gas Diving
MOUNT, TOM & GILLIAM, BRET *et al*. 2nd edn, Watersport, San Diego (1993)

An Introduction to Technical Diving
PALMER, ROB. Underwater World, Teddington (1994)

Diving Above Sea Level
WEINKE, BRUCE R. Best, Flagstaff (1999)

Cave/Cavern

Cave Diving [CDG Manual]
BALCOMBE, F.G. *et al* (eds). Mendip Publishing, Castle Cary (1990)

Basic Underwater Cave Surveying
BURGE, JOHN. NSS-CDS, Branford (1988)

Basic Cave Diving
EXLEY, SHECK. 5th edn, NSS-CDS, Branford (1986)

Caverns Measureless to Man
EXLEY, SHECK. Cave Books, St Louis (1994)

Cave Diving in Australia
LEWIS, IAN & STACE, PETER. Lewis, Adelaide (1980)

NSS Cave Diving Manual
PROSSER, J. JOSEPH & GREY, H.V. (eds). NSS-CDS, Branford (1998)

Cenote Carwash, Mexico

Awaiting an ice dive in Finland, with base-fed line already attached

The Art of Safe Cave Diving [NACD Manual]
Saltsman, Dayton (ed). NACD, Gainesville (1995)

NSS Cavern Diving Manual
Zumrick, John, Prosser, J. Joseph & Grey, H.V. NSS-CDS, Branford (1988)

Ice
Cold Water Diving
Heine, John N. Best, Flagstaff (1996)

Wreck
The Wreck Diving Manual
Bird, Lizzie. Crowood, Marlborough (1997)

The Last Dive
Chowdhury, Bernie. Headline, London (2000)

Advanced Wreck Diving Guide
Gentile, Gary. Cornell Maritime, Centreville (1988)

Primary Wreck Diving Guide
Gentile, Gary. GGP, Philadelphia (1998)

Beyond Sport Diving
Sheard, Bradley. Menasha Ridge, Birmingham, Alabama (1996)

Appendix B
Training Organisations

BSAC: British Sub-Aqua Club
Telford's Quay, South Pier Road, Ellesmere Port, CH65 4FL, UK
www.bsac.com

CDAA: Cave Divers Association of Australia
PO Box 290, North Adelaide, SA 5006, Australia
www.cavedivers.com.au

CDG: Cave Diving Group of Great Britain
Secretary: Dave Brock, 12 Carr Hill Road, Calverley, Pudsey, LS28 5PZ, UK
www.cavedivinggroup.org.uk

CMAS: Confédération Mondiale des Activités Subaquatiques (World Underwater Federation)
Viale Tiziano 74, 00196 Rome, Italy
www.cmas2000.org

GUE: Global Underwater Explorers
1110 South Main Street, High Springs,
FL 32643, USA
www.gue.com

IANTD: International Association of Nitrox and Technical Divers
9628 NE 2nd Avenue Suite D, Miami Shores,
FL 33138-2767, USA
www.iantd.com

NACD: National Association for Cave Diving
PO Box 14492, Gainesville, FL 32604, USA
www.safecavediving.com

NAUI: National Association of Underwater Instructors
PO Box 89789, Tampa, FL 33689-0413, USA
www.naui.com

NSS-CDS: National Speleological Society Cave Diving Section
PO Box 38057, Tallahassee, FL 32315-8057, USA
www.nsscds.com

PADI: Professional Association of Diving Instructors
PADI International Ltd, Unit 7, St Philips
Central, Albert Road, St Philips,
Bristol, BS2 0PD, UK
www.padi.com

TDI: Technical Diving International
18 Elm Street, Topsham, ME 04086, USA
www.tdisdi.com

Cave divers with back- and side-mounted cylinders at Wookey Hole, England

Appendix C
Calculating Gas Requirements

KNOWLEDGE of gas requirements is extremely important on all long or deep dives and it is particularly relevant for anyone contemplating cave diving (diving beyond the prescribed limits of cavern exploration) or wreck penetration at depth, as the configuration of a cave passage or wreck dictates the depth of the dive – an important consideration during exploration. The information presented in this appendix is generalised, but modern integrated dive computers generate precise information about breathing rates and this data can be used by divers to help plan future operations more accurately.

A diver resting at the surface breathes about 20 litres to 25 litres of air per minute. If stressed or working hard, consumption may rise to 60 litres a minute. However, while the volume of a diver's lungs remains constant, air and other breathing gases are compressed at depth. This means that, as depth increases, the 'surface' volume of air inhaled with each breath increases accordingly. For example, because the volume of air at the surface is compressed to half its volume at a pressure of 2 bar (10m depth), but each breath under pressure nevertheless requires the same volume of air to fill the lungs, the air supply will last for only half the duration. A cylinder at depth therefore supports a shorter duration dive than in shallow water.

One answer to this problem is to carry more air in the form of a larger cylinder or at an increased pressure. Cylinder volume is measured by filling it with water, giving a capacity in litres, while manufacturing constraints produce a maximum pressure that the cylinder can safely sustain. There are many different cylinder sizes available and the table indicates the 'free' volume of air which each of these examples would release on the surface at sea level (thus, under a pressure of 1 bar), calculated from the equation:

$$C = VW \times WP$$

where **C** is the contents in free litres of gas, **VW** is volume of the cylinder in litres of water, and **WP** is the working pressure of the cylinder in bar. Cylinders with a capacity of 3 litres and 5 litres are not manufactured with working pressures of 300 bar.

Cylinder volume and gas pressure

Size of cylinder (litres)	Pressure (bar)		
	200	*232*	*300*
3	600	696	–
5	1,000	1,160	–
7	1,400	1,624	2,100
10	2,000	2,320	3,000
12	2,400	2,784	3,600
15	3,000	3,480	4,500

Thus, a 15 litre cylinder pressurised to 200 bar contains 3,000 litres of free air, but if the same cylinder is filled to its maximum working pressure of 300 bar it would then contain 4,500 litres of free air.

From this data basic information for possible dive times can be calculated using the equation:

T = V/(Pa × R)

where **T** is the time in minutes, **V** is the volume in free litres, **Pa** is the absolute pressure in bar, and **R** is the ventilation volume in litres per minute (i.e. the breathing rate).

For example, a 10 litre cylinder filled at a pressure of 200 bar contains 2,000 litres of free air. With a breathing rate of 25 litres per minute this cylinder would sustain breathing at the surface (under a pressure of 1 bar) for approximately:

T = 2000/(1 × 25) = 80 minutes

Taking into account the effect of depth, where gas is compressed at the rate of 1 bar for every 10m, at 30m where the pressure is four times that at the surface the same cylinder would last for:

T = 2000/(4 × 25) = 20 minutes

If a diver is mentally stressed and breathes faster, this estimated duration could easily be halved. Calculate the dive duration if, instead of 25 litres per minute, air is breathed at 50 litres per minute (the increased rate being brought about by a change in current direction, for example) and ask yourself the question: Does this give my buddy and me enough air reserve in the event of an emergency?

Limited visibility in Mastic Point Blue Hole, Andros, Bahamas

Appendix D
Ice Diving

DIVING below ice can be spectacular, but the extremely low temperatures involved warrant the greatest respect. Temperatures on the surface, where you prepare for a dive, may lie well below zero and underwater it is rare for the temperature to exceed 3°C. In the sea this could be 1°C or lower, though at depth the water will be several degrees warmer. In particularly extreme conditions, for example when low surface temperatures are accompanied by strong winds, water temperatures may be –1°C or even –2°C and the viability of the dive should be carefully considered. Visibility beneath ice can also vary, from the spectacular translucent hues associated with the Antarctic where there is sometimes unlimited visibility, to perhaps only 1.5m in the Gulf of Fin-

Dragging diving gear on sleds across sea ice off the coast of Finland

land, which will affect the dive. This specialist area of activity requires considerable forethought and planning.

Hypothermia is a real concern. Drysuits, good quality gloves and the warmest undergarments available are of paramount importance. Using argon for suit inflation is extremely advantageous, as it helps retain warmth, and electrically heated undersuits are highly attractive. Suit heaters, such as those manufactured by Patco in the USA, may be used in semi-dry suits and it is clear that this technology will soon extend into many other environments.

Substantial external battery packs are required, but Canadian and Scandinavian divers have successfully used a normal canister light for a power source. This has proved sufficient for both heating and lighting, as under these extreme conditions it is not rational to undertake dives longer than 90 minutes. However, be wary of chemical heat packs. Although using these in a drysuit may feel comfortable at the surface, the increased partial pressure at depth can result in the packs burning hotter and faster than is desired and some divers have been burned. This aside, short dives without additional heating have been made using thick semi-dry suits.

An important first step in preventing hypothermia is to avoid becom-

Filming krill beneath
Antarctic pack ice

ing cold before the dive. All participants, divers and assistants alike, must
be well dressed and equipped. A wind chill factor greatly exacerbates low
temperatures and, to combat this, constructing a 'warm' shelter or wind-
break before changing is recommended. If the air temperature lies below
−10°C have hot water readily available to thaw attachments, zips and
other equipment immediately after the dive.

Regulators

Equipment must be appropriate for the prevalent conditions, in particular regulators. These must be reliable in extreme cold. Given that surface
temperatures may fall as low as −20°C, a wet regulator will freeze and
fail so a diver may only be able to breathe from his apparatus after submerging – and once submerged the diver dare not surface again, for example to relay a communication or collect another item of equipment.

Understanding the mechanics of a free-flowing regulator will help the diver select the appropriate equipment for ice diving. When a regulator is submerged it is subjected to near freezing conditions, but will continue to function unless its internal temperature drops below freezing. This can happen underwater if air flows through it at a high rate, as this cools the surrounding components. Thus, if a diver breathes rapidly and inflates a suit at the same time, the internal valve components might become over-chilled and ice crystals may form on the end of the piston.

Ice crystals can block the space between the piston and its high pressure seat, which stays open and allows additional air to escape through

Paul Heinerth exits from Ice Island Cave #4, Ross Sea, Antarctica

the first stage and pass downstream to the second stage. The second stage is (normally) a downstream valve, so the high pressure air forces it open and causes a free-flow under rapidly increasing pressure. Unchecked, this added pressure can exceed the specifications of the low pressure hose and rupture either it or the second stage. Under these conditions the sooner the regulator is turned off, the less ice can form in the first stage. If left to thaw under ambient water temperatures, regulators will usually work again when turned on, perhaps a minute or two later.

Second stages may also independently free-flow if ice jams the lever in an open position. This usually occurs when the second stage becomes wet and subsequently freezes on the surface. The drier the dive is started, the better.

A 'diaphragm design' regulator tends to be best choice for ice divers, as the unit is environmentally sealed and water cannot enter it. Piston regulators allow water to enter through ports in the first stage and are more likely to freeze. To counter this some Canadian divers inject silicon into the piston regulator ports to insulate them. More recent piston regulator designs have thermal insulating sleeves around the piston to decrease the likelihood of a free-flow.

Take great care to ensure that the breathing gas is dry. Moisture in the cylinders is perhaps the most common cause of regulators freezing. In the immediate pre-dive period the regulator's second stage should also be kept completely dry and not allowed contact with surface snow. Indeed, because it is not possible to breathe from the regulator until the diver is below water, testing should be completed well beforehand.

Communication

Communication between a diver and his or her attendant consists of a sequence of pulls upon a stout rope, to which the diver is firmly attached. A single pull by the attendant is a typical enquiry signal to ascertain if the diver is okay. If there is no response within a few seconds this leads to a diver's immediate recovery. The following signals are used by the Scandinavian sport-diving federations:

Signal	From diver	From attendant
One pull	OK	OK (is everything OK?)
Two pulls	Stop	Stop
Three pulls	Coming back/ take in rope	Come up
Four pulls or more: Emergency		

Cutting a triangular hole in ice. An ice-screw is used to make a small hole through which an ice-saw can cut the final hole. Here, surface snow is also being shovelled away to improve visibility beneath the ice

Other signalling systems may be used, for example those detailed in the *United States Navy Diving Manual*. As there may be significant differences, it is extremely important that everyone participating in an ice dive agrees completely on the signals that will be used. There must be no confusion.

Water entry

Where temperatures are extremely low and the ice cover is continuous, entry to the water is made via a relatively small hole cut with a specialist boring tool (more normally used by fishermen) and an ice-saw. Ideally, the ice should be over 50mm thick to support the weight of a fully equipped diver and to provide a strong, stable entry and exit from the water. In practice, the rule of thumb is that if you can pierce the ice using a sharp spike then it is too weak. Experience is important, but if the ice is only 25mm thick, this is marginal for weight-bearing.

In constructing the hole a triangle (or sometimes a square, though this is less convenient as there is poorer purchase for a diver leaving the water) with each side about 2m long is cut into the surface. For safety, wherever possible the dissected slabs of ice are moved at least 2m away.

As with other forms of overhead environment diving, the most common cause of fatality is that the individual becomes disorientated and lost. As an aid to route-finding, therefore, the surface near the hole may be marked with long radial furrows or 'spokes'. It is relatively easy to shovel snow aside and this allows more light to penetrate the ice. If it is sunny these furrows are seen fairly well from the underside and form additional guides back to the surface. It is also good practice to mark the position of the hole for the benefit and safety of other people who may subsequently walk on the ice (as a few millimetres of ice may later support a thin covering of snow, through which a walker can fall).

From more than a few metres from the entry point, even with guides in the surface snow, it is often difficult or impossible to see the hole in the ice and a line is essential. Ice diving organisa-

Hauling the cut block out of the hole. For safety, this will be dragged at least 2m away

Jill Heinerth diving in Fathom Five National Marine Park, Tobermory, Canada. This freshwater site contains an incredible concentration of wrecks

tions have different recommendations regarding the length and nature of rope that should be used, but the connection with the diver should use floating line with a minimum breaking strength of 300kg. The Finnish Sportdivers' Association suggests a maximum horizontal penetration of 20m from the hole, while 30m has been the traditional limit in Canada; the line obviously has to be long enough for the dive.

As the dive starts, an attendant, who is securely belayed, prepares to pay out line. For ease of handling it should be at least 8mm in diameter and, given the importance of the job, the attendant should wear warm, waterproof gloves. Constant vigilance is required to maintain the correct line tension with the diver. If a second diver is in the water at the same time, this requires that a separate attendant pays out the line or that the divers are physically connected by a short length of rope. Whatever approach is selected considerable care must be exercised to ensure that the ropes do not become entangled.

If the line is lost or becomes detached, the diver should immediately

Divers on sea ice near Helsinki, Finland, kit up for the dive using base-fed line. Note the use of a full face mask (below)

ascend and wait directly under the ice for a safety diver to arrive. To avoid being swept away in a current, Canadian divers suggest inserting a knife into the ice. In Finland it is customary that a fully equipped standby diver is connected to a rope that is twice as long as the diver's, so that the standby diver can cover a greater area than the diver is likely to be lost in. When searching, an immediate circular sweep is made just below the ice, hoping to locate the pinned diver. A bottom search is only commenced if this fails.

Emergency procedures

It is imperative that an ice diver is equipped with redundant regulators that are easy to reach in the event of a free-flow. In sub-zero conditions free-flows are common; the diver must be able to immediately turn off the gas supply and switch to an alternative regulator, while the first regulator slowly thaws. A free-flow scenario normally means the dive is aborted, but a malfunctioning regulator must still be turned off as a free-flow can easily develop sufficient pressure to explode a hose or second stage.

Advanced ice diving

Experienced ice divers who have received appropriate cave diving training may apply cave diving techniques under ice. Here, a weighted line is lowered from the surface hole and used by divers as a primary belay before reeling out, perhaps horizontally at depth to reach a tunnel in a wall. In Finland mines beneath ice have been dived at over 80m depth from a suspended line. If the line reaches the bottom this may aid recovery should contact be lost.

Some advanced cave divers have attempted dives inside glacial caves and icebergs. This very extreme form of the sport requires additional considerations. If strong currents are anticipated, ice tools such as

Preparing to dive (right and bottom) and the view of the hole, as seen by a returning diver

anchors (screws) and perhaps axes should be carried, as the slippery ice surface is impossible to grasp and a means of creating a handhold may be required. Ice screws are also extremely important during decompression as divers can fix themselves firmly in place and inflate their drysuits for extra warmth.

Ice caves are ever-changing environments. Shifting ice and calving glaciers are very dangerous places and, as with advanced diving in any overhead environment, training, experience and careful planning is essential.

Post-dive procedures

If repetitive ice dives are conducted over one or several days, great care must be taken to thoroughly dry all equipment. Second stages must be disassembled and attention paid to drying out suit valves. Failure to do so can result in an immediate free-flow if surface temperatures are below zero, even before a dive has commenced.

Appendix E
Wreck Diving

OPEN any dive magazine and the subject of wrecks abounds. Wrecks intrigue readers and wreck diving is often depicted in an encouraging light. Photographed in clear water, wrecks appear benign and the images naturally capture our interest; they seduce our common sense, fascinate and beckon. However, in reality, wrecks can present traps for the unwary. As with caves, they require a host of specialised equipment and techniques – they require skill, judgement and caution.

It does not take a lot of imagination to see that wrecks offer great potential for accidents. Compared with other areas of the overhead environment, wreck diving carries its own brand of danger. The surface environment may be hostile and, underwater, there are additional risks

such as becoming entangled in fishing lines or nets draped over a wreck, before it is even entered. Only if a wreck lies at a relatively shallow depth, and it is open with an unobstructed ascent, can such dangers be considered minor.

When the structure is largely intact and there are openings large enough to swim through, wreck penetration is much more serious. Because ambient light diminishes with depth (especially where visibility is poor), divers routinely carry a light. It is ironic that the act of having a light can lead to divers being enticed inside a structure – purely to 'see what's there'. Wreck penetration should be regarded as a more committing undertaking than this, requiring thorough preparation, planning and training. Many leading wreck divers have completed cave diving courses

Diving on mixed gases, Brad Froggat's exhaust bubbles disturb silt in the confined engine room of the wreck of the US tanker *Illinois*

Deep wrecks in the North Atlantic Ocean can
produce romantic images, as with the bow
section of the First World War ocean liner
Justicia. At 70m depth, internal exploration is a
serious undertaking

specifically to further their wreck activities.

Wrecks in deep water require rigorous attention to detail. Beyond 30m depth narcosis will impair judgement and using mixed gases, or a rebreather, may be essential. Such considerations clearly have a profound impact on equipment configuration and technique. All divers must be wary of depth when exploring a wreck. It is possible that if the seabed is soft, or silt has accumulated against the side of the structure, that the inside of a hull may be significantly deeper than the outside, particularly within the hold.

The stability of a wreck should always be questioned. Even swimming under a piece of wreckage is dangerous. Hanging doors, walls, ceilings or attachments may be so poorly supported that they collapse due to disturbance from the diver's exhaust bubbles or fin movements. There have been a number of instances where divers have been trapped by a moving structure, either pinning the diver to the floor or seabed or by blocking the exit. It is significant that expeditions to the *Britannic* (sister ship of the *Titanic*) – which lies at a depth of 120m – may now only gain a licence for penetration if divers use rebreathers, a deliberate attempt by the wreck's owner to protect the site from damage resulting from exhaust bubbles.

Joanne Fox contemplates entering the wreck of the *Illinois*, sunk during the First World War by a German U-boat. Strong tidal currents at a depth of 70m in the English Channel means that careful planning is essential

If silt is disturbed inside a wreck the natural light of open water is lost and inexperienced divers are therefore advised to remain outside. Light intensity also decreases naturally at dusk and when cloud cover develops, and these factors – combined with the threat of silt disturbance – produce a recipe for disaster. Diving any wreck at night is a totally different, more serious undertaking and many deep wreck dives are conducted within daylight hours, if only due to the constraint of lengthy decompression schedules. A boat's captain requires daylight to keep an eye on the surface marker buoy marking the location of a diver drifting free in a tidal current. Wreck diving at night is therefore normally only undertaken on shallow inshore sites.

A wreck can accumulate quantities of fine silt very soon after sinking and, without a foolproof method of returning to open water, entering any structure is clearly dangerous. Divers, attracted by light streaming through portholes or deck skylights, have been lured into a false sense of security and paid the price by discovering too late that there was no escape route. Internal plate glass windows have also proved deceptive; indeed, light will pass through openings which may be restrictive or impossible for a diver to negotiate. Almost certainly, the best exit is the original point of entry.

Knowledge and wreck diving experience go a long way to making dives safe. Wreck navigation is crucial, especially in the predictably low visibility that is normally encountered over the course of what may be a complex route. As in caves, no method of route-finding is failure proof and using multiple navigational techniques, employed as conditions dictate, is important. Previous experience of the wreck is invaluable, combined with a good memory and simple identification of specific landmarks.

Divers should study ship plans and familiarise themselves with its layout, counting portholes or doorways on the way in as an aid to navigation. Strobe lights or lightsticks (chemically activated, disposable lights)

can be set down at critical navigation points. A compass may be useful, but only if you are familiar with the wreck plan and know the direction that you need to travel – and even then its accuracy may be suspect, given the proximity of so much metal. General awareness of the natural lines of the wreck, such as a prominent pipe or cable, or the basic design of that class of vessel, is always useful, as is the knowledge of the precise depth of key features. Lastly – a penetration line is invaluable (see Chapter 4).

The pump house of the US tanker *Illinois* (top). A dive which follows the ladder down to the interior depths near the keel is a major commitment.

The *Osprey* (lower) lies on her port side at –75m; with walls now acting as floors and ceilings and fixtures in disarray, divers can become disoriented. Penetrating wrecks demands that strict overhead environment techniques are used

There is considerable debate about the best use of lines within wrecks and, indeed, there are those who state that a line should not be used at all. These individuals believe that it is far better to learn your way around the wreck based upon experience gained during a series of progressive penetrations and a close study of the ship's plan. This is hardly a tenable argument, for in a moment of distraction a diver may become completely disorientated inside a dark space, perhaps in total blackout, within a ship that may be lying on her side. Diving into a wreck without laying line is only recommended where there is lots of ambient light.

A classic, much-heralded site where lines are not generally used is the Italian liner the *Andrea Doria*, lying 75m below the surface many kilometres off the north-east coast of the USA. Here, divers have made extensive use of strobe lights and lightsticks to mark prominent points on the exit route. Clearly, this approach is dependent upon an environment that has minimal silt, or at the very least one in which visibility rapidly clears. Such wrecks are few and far between and even on the *Doria* a dozen deaths have occurred, four within the wreck attributed directly to the overhead environment.

Only a well-positioned guideline, installed by an experienced lead diver, provides any guarantee of a safe exit. Before entering a wreck while laying a line practise using an appropriate reel in a 'safe' environment. Reel design is important. Ratchet-type reels, which let out a small amount of line before locking, or which need to be held open to permit free-spooling, are fairly easy to use and prevent too much line from being accidentally deployed. However, if the ratchet engages unexpectedly the reel can be snatched from your hand and ratchets also form a failure point that can cause jamming. This type of reel, typically used with a surface marker buoy, is not easy to operate within a wreck and there have been many instances of failure and jamming. Many agencies therefore advise against their use for line-laying, particularly in an overhead environment. Free-running reels, equipped with a locking mechanism, are more versatile and safe.

Divers should not be tempted into a wreck because they happen to have a reel. Penetration of any wreck is not a spur of the moment activity; it is not the place to discover limitations with equipment or technique. If a penetration dive is planned then a second, redundant reel should always be carried to ensure that you always have a reel with which

An unknown wreck in the Red Sea. In warm water, the prospect of sport diving on a wreck is an attractive venture made more inviting by tour companies and magazines. However, conditions inside can soon change from clear water to zero visibility – training and correct technique is essential to launch a surface marker buoy.

Wrecks usually provide a wealth of good belay points, but these should always be checked for integrity and sharp edges. The use of relatively thin 'technical' line is the norm in this environment, but even heavy-gauge line may be severed by a rusting metal edge. Divers must consider anything that may cut or compromise the line if it is accidentally pulled and act accordingly; in particular, excessively tight lines may be more susceptible to rubbing (perhaps under the influence of currents, wreck movement or the motion of a diver moving along it).

Before entering the structure it is prudent to secure the line outside the wreck in open water, then make a second belay just inside. At a popular venue this extra precaution, along with the placement of a dated dive slate, provides extra security should another diver (perhaps from a second boat) tamper with the line or accidentally become caught in it while passing and inadvertently jeopardise a safe exit. If the first belay is at the entrance to the wreck and this is disturbed, there is no longer any safe route to open water.

When laying line inside a wreck avoid criss-crossing any passageway, unless absolutely necessary. A line that changes sides inevitably means that on a multi-dive project divers keep crossing back and fore and, depending upon the size of the passage or the belay positions, this adds to the risk of entanglement or severance. Divers will probably have to repeatedly swap hands and this increases difficulties, particularly in poor visibility. Don't forget that using a line increases the time required for the dive, both in laying it going in and removing it while exiting.

In bad visibility, to ensure that a diver never strays far from the entry point, a very basic technique is to use a base-fed line paid out by a buddy outside the wreck. However, this technique is limited: communication is problematic and any change in direction made by the lead diver risks pulling the line into a line trap (see p44), or against a sharp surface whereupon a sudden movement by either person might sever a thin line.

In the majority of wrecks silt is the major hazard encountered by divers. Though wrecks are of a limited extent compared with most caves, negotiating what may be a complex, three-dimensional maze-like structure is nevertheless stressful. If the wreck is deep or set on its side and the visibility is low, this constitutes a very serious dive where ceilings and floors may become walls and the potential for confusion is huge. Divers must be completely self-sufficient and should regard exploration as a solo undertaking.

There is little doubt that divers themselves create most visibility problems and only a few fin strokes may reduce visibility to near zero. Then, even the most powerful lighting units are rendered useless. Unless you are in touch contact, your buddy is another potential source of stress (see Chapter 7). In conditions of stress the most important course of action is to restore calm. Maintain position, take a few breaths and analyse the situation – more often than not it is the perception of a problem, rather than the problem itself, that leads to high stress. Stop, think and control your emotions before reacting. If there is a current, it will slowly disperse the silt-cloud: stay still, slow your breathing rate and wait.

Wrecks frequently contain suspended wires and cables that are easy to become caught in – and cannot be cut with a knife (scissor-type wire-cutters are a far better choice for this situation). In such an area extreme caution is important; prevention is better than cure and streamlined equipment is essential. Stage cylinders should be dropped and securely attached to the line just outside the wreck, rather than risking excessive clutter and possible entanglement in a restricted area with low visibility. The timing of dives is critical, especially in strong tidal water; slack wa-

ter is short-lived and swimming against a rising current while heavily equipped is not a viable option.

Collecting souvenirs has always been a significant feature of wreck diving. Attitude is crucial as, when it comes to artefacts, some people become ego-driven to recover what they perceive to be valuable 'treasure'. Possessing an item, such as a crested plate or piece of porcelain from a famous liner, becomes a personal statement among peers that the diver has reached a specific part of the wreck. There is little doubt that such an acquisition infers status in the eyes of less experienced divers.

Undertaking this, or any other activity within a wreck, requires additional equipment and planning. More gas is consumed, and special care and very close attention must be given to the course of time, often under stressful conditions. Deaths have been caused by this quest for souvenirs, a somewhat embarrassing and fortunately diminishing aspect of the activity today. Commercial and salvage divers may already be well versed in this type of work, but for amateur divers one simple approach for avoiding visibility problems when digging or moving wreckage is to orient yourself toward the exit before you begin to dig, and to excavate into the current, not with it. As in cave diving, at the sharp end of such a project a huge amount of support is required just to place one diver inside a deep wreck.

Some wrecks are afforded protection by law; though divers may be allowed to visit these sensitive sites, it is only on a look-but-don't-touch basis. Divers may not enter such wrecks, disturb them or remove any artefacts and severe penalties may be imposed if these rules are ignored. Always ensure the correct permissions are in place before undertaking a dive.

Wreck diving can be very rewarding but, as with all other incursions into the overhead environment, preparation and planning, along with an understanding of the specific dangers involved, are necessary to ensure a safe and enjoyable dive.

The wreck of the dreadnought HMS *Audacious* lies upside down in the North Atlantic, enticing divers into a labyrinth of passages at –67m

Appendix F
Glossary

Words in *italics* cross-reference within this glossary

air: Composition by percentage: nitrogen 78.084%, oxygen 20.946%, argon 0.934%, carbon dioxide 0.0335%, rare gases 0.0025% (consisting primarily of neon, helium, krypton, hydrogen and xenon). For most practical purposes air is represented as 79% nitrogen and 21% oxygen.

air pocket: An enclosed gas-filled space between the water surface and the roof of a cave or mine. The gas may be depleted of oxygen or be toxic and thus may not support life.

ATA: Atmospheres Absolute: a measure of air pressure in pounds per square inch (psi: 1 atmosphere = 14.7 psi). In Europe pressure is measured in the metric equivalent, *bar*.

back-mounted BC: Buoyancy compensator worn on the diver's back (synonymous with wings).

back-up light: A secondary light unit, carried in case the primary light fails.

bar: Metric unit of pressure measurement (for bar to *ATA* conversion, multiply by 0.986).

BC: Buoyancy compensator: a gas-filled device for adjusting a diver's buoyancy underwater.

bedding plane: Boundary layer separating two rock beds; a characteristically low and wide bedding plane passage may form on this boundary.

blue hole: Flooded cave system, at or below sea level (typically in the Bahamas and Caribbean). These caves were formed by fresh water when sea levels were lower.

bottom time: The time from the beginning of a dive to the arrival at the deepest *decompression stop*.

bubble check: Equipment check, normally undertaken by a diver's buddy, to ensure that the breathing apparatus has no leaks.

bump-and-go system: A touch-contact system used in low visibility when divers cannot maintain normal communication, also known as the touch-and-go method. The leading diver swims for a specified distance or time, then waits for his or her buddy to catch up. Once the second diver re-establishes physical contact, the lead diver continues.

carbonic acid: A weak acid formed when rainwater absorbs carbon dioxide (CO_2) from the atmosphere.

cavern zone: Within the diving world, an area of submerged cave or mine lit by natural sunlight which may be dived using relatively normal equipment, after suitable training.

cenote: A flooded cave system in Mexico.

circuit: A dive with the same entrance and exit point, but where a portion requires one-way travel (cf. *traverse*).

clothes peg/pin (UK/USA): A temporary line marker, normally attached to the line at the safe 'out' side of a line junction. Generally marked with the owner's name.

CNS: Central Nervous System: the brain and spinal cord.

column: A solid pillar of rock formed by the connection of a stalactite and a stalagmite.

cu.ft.: Cubic feet: a unit of measurement of volume. To convert cu.ft. to *litres* multiply by 28.32.

danglies: Items of equipment hanging from the diver's harness in an unstreamlined manner. These slow the diver's progress through the water and are prone to entanglement.

decompression stop: A stop at a specified depth for a specified time during an ascent, to allow time for decompression.

decorations: Speleothems, such as stalactites or stalagmites, found in a cave passage.

DPV: Diver Propulsion Vehicle: an underwater scooter.

drop weights: Lead weights used at the start of a dive but removed at (say) 10m depth. At the close of the dive these are picked up again to offset increased positive buoyancy and thus they are sometimes referred to as decompression weights.

dual valve manifold: A rigid valve assembly which connects two back-mounted cylinders (also called a cross-over manifold). There are two high-pressure valve outlets, allowing two regulators to simultaneously access the total gas supply. In the event of a regulator failure the other regulator can still access all the gas – an advantage over separate (independent) systems, where a faulty regulator would lose access to the air in its attached cylinder. See also *isolation manifold*.

EAD: see *equivalent air depth*.

EANx: Enriched Air Nitrox: *nitrox* containing greater than 21% oxygen (as found in *air*), though commonly still referred to as nitrox. Rather than creating a pure mix composed solely of nitrogen and oxygen, Enriched Air Nitrox is made by adding compressed air to a cylinder containing a specified percentage of oxygen. This produces nitrox 'enriched' with the trace gases normally found in air – in the same relative amounts, but in reduced concentration. The oxygen content may be indicated by adding the actual percentage figure of oxygen, eg. EANx 32 contains 32% oxygen.

equivalent air depth (EAD): A dive using nitrox or another mixed gas decreases the diver's exposure to nitrogen and thus decreases the decompression obligation. The equivalent air depth is the calculated depth that the diver would have been able to attain with the same nitrogen exposure, if diving on air.

flutter kick: The most common fin stroke used by divers, whereby both legs alternately perform the same motion. It is perhaps the most natural finning action and is particularly powerful for forward motion. However, the downward thrust in the water causes silt disturbance and other, or modified, finning actions are therefore preferred. The modified flutter kick, for example, uses bent knees, producing a significant improvement.

frog kick: A fin stroke where each leg performs a mirror image of the other at the same time, virtually the same action as in breaststroke swimming. It is an extremely powerful action which, given that it drives the water horizontally backwards rather than downwards, produces little silt disturbance. This stroke is often the primary method of swimming in the overhead environment.

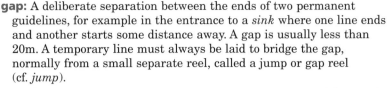

gap: A deliberate separation between the ends of two permanent guidelines, for example in the entrance to a *sink* where one line ends and another starts some distance away. A gap is usually less than 20m. A temporary line must always be laid to bridge the gap, normally from a small separate reel, called a jump or gap reel (cf. *jump*).

halocline: A layer of water with significantly impaired visibility at the boundary where fresh water and underlying salt water meet and mix.

heliair: A helium and air mixture, typically produced by partially filling a cylinder with helium and topping it up with air.

heliox: A gas mixture consisting of helium and oxygen, mixed in differing proportions depending upon the *maximum operating depth*, and designed to reduce the narcotic effects of nitrogen. Heliox mixtures used for diving often contain a lower percentage of oxygen than is found in air because of the increasing toxicity of oxygen with depth.

hydrogen sulphide: A toxic, water-soluble gas (H_2S) formed by the decay of certain organic materials and characterised by a rotten egg smell. Normally occurring in a thin 'sulphur layer' of limited extent, it causes divers few adverse effects. Its main significance is that the sulphur layer will not transmit surface light.

hypercapnia: An excessive concentration of carbon dioxide dissolved in the blood, causing the blood pH to fall. Excessive carbon dioxide levels lead to drowsiness and confusion, and this has been linked to drowning due to loss of consciousness at depth.

hypoxia: A condition where the body is acutely short of oxygen.

isolation manifold: An addition to a *dual valve manifold* is a central valve hand wheel, allowing the cylinders as well as the regulators to be isolated if required.

joint: A vertical crack in limestone.

jump: A deliberate separation between two permanent guidelines to make a clear distinction between a line running along the main route and lines installed in side tunnels. A jump may be as short as 1m. A temporary line must always be laid to bridge the jump (normally from a small separate reel, called a jump or gap reel), making a T-junction in the line (cf. *gap*).

karst window: A classic limestone landscape is known as karst; a karst window is a diveable site on the surface giving entry to a flooded cave system below (cf. *sink* and *resurgence*, which imply flowing water).

lava tube: Cave found in volcanic areas, formed by the flow of molten lava. Tubes are generally close to the surface and normally entered through a roof collapse.

line arrow: Small, rigid, plastic triangle placed on a guideline to point towards the exit. It may be a permanent (pointing towards the nearest exit) or a temporary marker (to be removed on the outward journey).

line trap: A constriction which may be impossible for a diver to pass through but where a guideline may unintentionally have become lodged. Low, meandering bedding planes are particularly problematic.

litre: A metric unit of measurement of gas or liquid volume. To convert litres to *cu.ft.* multiply by 0.03531.

manifold: See *dual valve manifold*.

maximum operating depth (MOD): The maximum depth attainable by a diver, determined by the partial pressure of oxygen the diving gas contains.

mixed gas: Any breathing mixture other than compressed air. The most common are *heliox*, *nitrox* and *trimix*, all of which may be blended differently depending upon the requirements of the dive.

MOD: See *maximum operating depth*.

nitrogen narcosis: The progressive impairment of mental capacity, brought about by a high partial pressure of nitrogen.

nitrox: A breathable gas mixture consisting primarily of nitrogen and oxygen (also commonly used to refer to Enriched Air Nitrox: *EANx*).

octopus: Twin regulators drawing air through the same first stage and cylinder and therefore *redundancy* is not complete.

OTU: Oxygen Tolerance Units are used to track exposure to the cumulative effects of oxygen during multi-day diving operations.

phreatic tube: The phreatic zone is a permanently flooded area below the water table (unlike the vadose zone, where water flows beneath an air surface). A cave passage forming in this submerged phreas is termed a phreatic tube and is typically cylindrical.

PPO$_2$: Partial pressure of oxygen in a breathing mix.

psi: Pounds per square inch: a unit of pressure measurement. The metric equivalent is the *bar*.

redundancy: Back-up equipment is carried in the event of failure or loss of any critical item during a dive; the principle is termed redundancy. Each item must be totally separate and able to be used as a full replacement (cf. *octopus*).

referencing: A memory-stimulating exercise. The diver pays close attention to the environment on the inward journey to memorise as much detail as possible, as this may prove invaluable in safely retracing the same route.

resurgence: A point where an underground river or stream rises to the surface (synonymous with spring).

Rimbach system: A system for touch contact communication. Both divers are positioned in single file on the same side of the line. The rear diver holds the forward diver's arm or leg with one hand while holding the guideline with the other. Pushing indicates go forward, squeezing indicates stop and pulling indicates back up or reverse.

Rule of Thirds: The principle of using a third of a cylinder's air on an inward dive and a third on the return, holding the final third in reserve for emergencies. Also known as the Thirds Rule. Dives of potentially greater difficulty or when a scooter is used may require a Rule of Fourths or Sixths, where a greater proportion of air in the cylinder is retained as a reserve.

S-drill: Safety drill: a drill or exercise where divers rehearse air-sharing, also involving signalling, selecting an appropriate regulator and swimming in tandem for a short distance. The whole team should participate.

safety stop: A brief pause, perhaps for several minutes, in the final stages of ascent on a no-decompression dive. It increases the safety margin, thereby lessening the chance of a decompression incident after regaining the surface.

sink: A point on the surface where water enters the ground or a cave. When the sink (or sinkhole) is flooded it may be termed a siphon, typically in the USA. In French the term siphon means *sump*.

siphon: A flooded *sink* (USA); a *sump* (French).

snoopy loop: A stretchy, rubber loop of varying size normally fashioned from a discarded bicycle or car inner tube and immensely useful for line belaying, streamlining equipment and general problem-solving.

speleology: The scientific study and exploration of caves and related features.

spring: See *resurgence*.

streamlining: Arranging personal diving equipment to minimise resistance while swimming and to lessen the chance of items catching on rock walls.

sump: A water-filled section of cave passage (in French: siphon).

tannic water: Tannin-stained water; tannin derives from decaying leaves and other organic debris, turning the water brown.

task loading: Where a diver undertakes more or increasingly complex tasks, producing increased energy expenditure (either physical or mental) and in turn a greater predisposition to stress.

traverse: A one-way journey from one entrance of a cave or mine to another some distance away (cf. *circuit*).

trim: The diver's balance or position in the water, variously described as head up, level or head down. Good trim generally denotes a good swimming position with minimum silt disturbance.

trimix: Breathing gas consisting of nitrogen, helium and oxygen, used on deep dives to decrease the effects of *nitrogen narcosis*.

turnaround: The point where the inward dive is terminated. This should be planned and normally depends on factors such as air consumption, time, depth and distance.

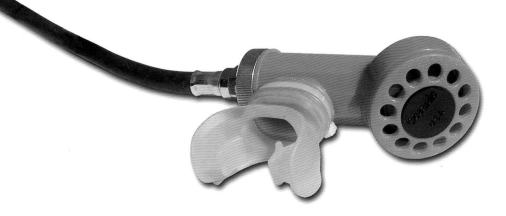

Index

Rick Stanton
with scooter